POPULAR MUSIC, STARS AND STARDOM

POPULAR MUSIC, STARS AND STARDOM

EDITED BY STEPHEN LOY, JULIE RICKWOOD
AND SAMANTHA BENNETT

Published by ANU Press
The Australian National University
Acton ACT 2601, Australia
Email: anupress@anu.edu.au

Available to download for free at press.anu.edu.au

A catalogue record for this book is available from the National Library of Australia

ISBN (print): 9781760462123
ISBN (online): 9781760462130

WorldCat (print): 1039732304
WorldCat (online): 1039731982

DOI: 10.22459/PMSS.06.2018

This title is published under a Creative Commons Attribution-NonCommercial-NoDerivatives 4.0 International (CC BY-NC-ND 4.0).

The full licence terms are available at creativecommons.org/licenses/by-nc-nd/4.0/legalcode

Cover design by Fiona Edge and layout by ANU Press

This edition © 2018 ANU Press

All chapters in this collection have been subjected to a double-blind peer-review process, as well as further reviewing at manuscript stage.

Contents

Acknowledgements vii

Contributors ix

1. Popular Music, Stars and Stardom: Definitions, Discourses, Interpretations 1
   Stephen Loy, Julie Rickwood and Samantha Bennett

2. Interstellar Songwriting: What Propels a Song Beyond Escape Velocity? 21
   Clive Harrison

3. A Good Black Music Story? Black American Stars in Australian Musical Entertainment Before 'Jazz' 37
   John Whiteoak

4. 'You're Messin' Up My Mind': Why Judy Jacques Avoided the Path of the Pop Diva 55
   Robin Ryan

5. Wendy Saddington: Beyond an 'Underground Icon' 73
   Julie Rickwood

6. Unsung Heroes: Recreating the Ensemble Dynamic of Motown's Funk Brothers 95
   Vincent Perry

7. When Divas and Rock Stars Collide: Interpreting Freddie Mercury and Montserrat Caballé's *Barcelona* 115
   Eve Klein

8. Intimacy, Authenticity and 'Worlding' in Beyoncé's Star Project 137
   Phoebe Macrossan

Index 153

Acknowledgements

The authors would like to thank Emily Hazlewood and the editorial staff at ANU Press, as well as the members of the ANU Press Humanities & Creative Arts Editorial Board, for their work in bringing this book to fruition. We would also like to extend our thanks and appreciation to the anonymous peer reviewers, those who reviewed individual contributions and those who were engaged by ANU Press to review. The feedback we received on both individual chapters and the draft manuscript was vital in developing our ideas. We would also like to extend our gratitude to both ANU Press and the ANU Humanities Research Centre for their generous financial support of this project, particularly Professor Will Christie. We also thank Fiona Edge of DesignEdge ACT for her creation of the cover image for this volume. Finally, we would like to extend special thanks to each of the authors for their innovative and insightful contributions to the continuing discourse on stars and stardom in popular music.

Contributors

Samantha Bennett is a sound recordist, guitarist and Associate Professor in music at The Australian National University. She is the author of two monographs, *Modern Records, Maverick Methods* and *Peepshow*, a 33 1/3 series edition (both Bloomsbury Academic). Samantha's journal articles are published in *Popular Music, Popular Music and Society, The Journal of Popular Music Studies* and *IASPM@journal*.

Dr Clive Harrison has performed with a stunning list of Australian contemporary artists, and has recorded over 98 albums, 50 films and 3,500 commercials. His 2016 PhD thesis was in creativity, multiple intelligences and songwriting, and he is the Deputy Director, Academic Affairs, at the Australian Institute of Music.

Dr Eve Klein is a music technologist and popular music scholar, an operatic mezzo soprano and a composer. Eve works at the University of Queensland's School of Music as Program Convenor of Popular Music and Technology. Her current research explores classical music recording practices, popular–classical music hybridity, and technology-enabled performance.

Dr Stephen Loy is lecturer in music at the ANU School of Music, and has convened courses in music theory and aural skills, critical and historical musicology, and popular music studies. He has published on the music of Louis Andriessen and Led Zeppelin.

Phoebe Macrossan is a PhD candidate at the University of NSW, and a tutor in film studies at Queensland University of Technology. Her thesis examines the utopian modalities of screen song across film, television and music video. She is a co-founder of the Sydney Screen Studies Network and the Postgraduate Executive Member for the Screen Studies Association of Australia and Aotearoa/New Zealand.

Dr Vincent Perry is a Brisbane-based drummer, record producer and avid collector of vintage instruments and recording gear. In late 2017, Vincent received his PhD from Queensland Conservatorium, Griffith University. He is currently a sessional lecturer at JMC Academy where he teaches music, audio and entertainment business units.

Dr Julie Rickwood is a music and performance researcher and practitioner based in Canberra, Australia. Located at The Australian National University, her research has concentrated on popular music and community choirs exploring intersections with music making such as cross-cultural exchange and common ground, gender, identity, place, heritage and the environment.

Dr Robin Ryan studied music at the University of Western Australia, the University of Washington and Monash University. She published on indigenous and popular music topics while a Research Fellow of Macquarie University, Sydney (2001–05). Robin currently conducts ecomusicological research through the Western Australian Academy of Performing Arts, Edith Cowan University.

John Whiteoak is an Adjunct Professor in the Sir Zelman Cowen School of Music, Monash University. He was co-editor for the *Currency Companion to Music and Dance in Australia* (2003) and has published widely on jazz related topics, including *Playing Ad Lib, Improvisatory Music In Australia, 1836–1970* (1999).

1

Popular Music, Stars and Stardom: Definitions, Discourses, Interpretations

Stephen Loy, Julie Rickwood and Samantha Bennett

What do we mean when we talk of 'pop stars' or 'rock stars'? What do we seek to convey when we describe a particular performer as a 'pop star'? The use of the term 'star' to describe an individual's outstanding achievement within a particular field may be traced as far back as the early nineteenth century, when the term was used in popular discourse concerning those who excelled in their fields, particularly in the theatre and the sporting arena (Oxford English Dictionary Online, 2016). The term gained a particular currency, however, with its use in describing the most prominent and popular actors of the Hollywood film studios during the first half of the twentieth century. In this sense, the application of the word star connotes publicly recognised success, and it is often in this manner that we apply the terms 'pop star' or 'rock star' to acclaimed performers of popular music.

However, our identification and veneration of stars, either of stage or screen, is demonstrative of a complex web of social and cultural processes, which raises other questions, and invites comparisons with notions of fame and celebrity. In particular, the way a star's persona may be understood as both commercial commodity and an individualised, personalised reflection of broader social or cultural meanings, invites questions of the ways in which the star becomes 'an object of cultural politics' (Gledhill, 1991, p. xiv). Here, notions of stardom intersect and overlap with those of celebrity.

Whereas stardom is taken to derive from professional success and its popular recognition, celebrity as a form of fame is more contested, particularly in terms of its perceived value. Fred Inglis, in his *A Short History of Celebrity*, makes a historical distinction between renown, which is governed by and attributed to individuals based on position or achievement, and the more recent phenomenon of celebrity, which he argues is more transitory (Inglis, 2010, pp. 4–5). This sense that celebrity may be disconnected from professional success in a field is further emphasised by Graeme Turner, who argues that 'the modern celebrity may claim no special achievements other than the attraction of public attention' (Turner, 2014, p. 3). Similarly, Sean Redmond and Su Holmes note the at times derogatory connotations of the term 'celebrity', which places it in a hierarchical relationship with the notion of 'stardom': 'the concept of the "star" [is] positioned above the concept of the celebrity—with its persistent association with fame as more ubiquitous, and thus devalued, currency' (Redmond and Holmes, 2007, p. 8).

While the term 'star' continues to be used to describe 'those known for a public role in a particular profession' (Redmond and Holmes, 2007, p. 9), and, therefore, may be distinguished from the notion of celebrity as one who is 'well-known for their well-knownness' (Boorstin, 1971, p. 58), Marsha Orgeron has noted the 'categorical slipperiness' between these terms, and others such as 'personality' and 'superstar', with meanings shifting in response to developments in culture and its depiction (Orgeron, 2008, 190). Despite these particulars of definition, the role that stars play in the pervasive cultural, commercial and social processes connected with popular culture mandates a consideration of the phenomenon in the context of these broader issues. Indeed, the development of academic disciplines around stardom and celebrity reflects the diversity of approaches that may be taken to its investigation.

Critical discourses concerning stardom and celebrity date from the 1970s, arising initially as a component of the emergent film studies of the period. It was in examinations of the roles played by stars within the film industry, and their significance to audiences, that the field has its genesis. In particular, Richard Dyer's book *Stars*, first published in 1979, proved a seminal work in the establishment of approaches to issues of stardom as

1. DEFINITIONS, DISCOURSES, INTERPRETATIONS

they related to the commercial and social processes of the film industry. Dyer's was the first critical study of stardom in cinema that sought to interrogate how stars, as images projected within film and via other 'media texts' and intersecting with their functional role as characters within films, through both their on-screen characters and off-screen personae, informed and helped shape social and cultural ideas (Dyer, 1998, p. 1). Dyer's critique of the 'star image' (Dyer, 1998, p. 129) and its role in the creation of sociocultural meaning was further developed in his subsequent work *Heavenly Bodies: Film Stars and Society*, in which he focused on the significant figures of Marilyn Monroe, Paul Robeson and Judy Garland to explore the interrelationship of star construction and audience reception in the creation of cultural meaning (Dyer, 2004).

Dyer's approach to the critique of stardom through the notion of the 'star image' as a 'media text' set a critical frame for the exploration of the social function of stardom within the entertainment industries, influencing many subsequent studies. While acknowledging this debt, and firmly grounded in the discipline of film studies, Christine Gledhill's 1991 collection, *Stardom: Industry of Desire*, brought together studies by a range of contributors from across the disciplines of cultural studies, media and communication studies, gender studies and politics, emphasising a belief in the study of stardom as necessarily interdisciplinary. Gledhill (1991) writes in the introduction to the collection:

> The star challenges analysis in the way it crosses boundaries: a product of mass culture, but retaining theatrical concerns with acting, performance and art; an industrial marketing device, but a signifying element in films; a social sign, carrying cultural meanings and ideological values, which expresses the intimacies of individual personality, inviting desire and identification; an emblem of national celebrity, founded on the body, fashion and personal style; a product of capitalism and the ideology of individualism, yet a site of contest by marginalised groups; a figure consumed for his or her personal life, who competes for allegiance with statesmen and politicians. (p. xiii)

This eloquent outline of the complex issues at play in stardom's social and cultural functioning reflects the ways in which discourses in studies of stardom and celebrity have subsequently developed, with a burgeoning of the field into a broad range of disciplines, particularly since the turn of the millennium.

Orgeron identifies three critical theoretical directions, which encompass much of the subsequent interdisciplinary diversity of the work conducted within stardom studies during the past two decades. Noting that 'the scholarship about media celebrity is diffuse in terms of both its breadth and its disciplinary focus', Orgeron identifies the key fields as 'the work of stardom', approaches that further develop Dyer's notion of the 'star text', and studies that examine the role of stars within issues of 'identity politics' (Orgeron 2008, pp. 201–202).

The 'work of stardom', as described by Orgeron, extends far beyond the labour of that which is required of the star in the production of a film or other creative artefact. Indeed, 'movie stars are actors well beyond the limited time they spend in front of the cameras', and the requirement that the star continue the presentation of a public persona extends far beyond their formal acting work (Orgeron, 2008, p. 202). Despite this being a key element of the perpetuation of stardom, Orgeron argues that it is an aspect of the field that is rarely examined, with a preference for the consideration of stars as celebrity icons taking precedence. Despite this, in recent decades analyses of the labour processes that go into the production and support of the star image have further developed this area of stardom studies. The work of Graeme Turner, in particular his *Understanding Celebrity* (2014) and, with Frances Bonner and P. David Marshall, *Fame Games* (2000), interrogates the elements of the celebrity industries that create and support the projection of stars and celebrities, uncovering aspects of these industries that 'actively mask their own activities' (Turner, 2014, p. 44).

Studies that develop Dyer's 'media text' approach focus on the industry construction of stars, and how the images and personae created are employed to influence audience consumption and reception. 'The construction and consumption of star promotion are necessarily distinct categories, each revealing more, perhaps, about their maker and consumer than about the stars themselves' (Orgeron, 2008, pp. 205–206). Therefore, studies in this vein combine aspects of the fields of economics, media and communication studies with sociological studies of audience behaviour and reception. An example of the development of stardom studies from this perspective is the work of Christine Geraghty. In 'Re-examining Stardom: Questions of Texts, Bodies and Performance' (2000), Geraghty further develops the study of star images through

1. DEFINITIONS, DISCOURSES, INTERPRETATIONS

the interrogation of the ways in which stars create cultural meaning, examining distinctions between these processes when considering the star as a celebrity as opposed to a professional and a performer.

The interdisciplinary nature of stardom studies is further demonstrated by those studies that investigate issues of what Orgeron describes as 'identity politics'. Orgeron characterises these works as focusing on the 'human' aspects of stardom, in contrast to those that focus on the industrial mechanisms of stardom (Orgeron, 2008, p. 209). The multiplicity of these studies concerning issues of gender, race, ethnicity, sexuality and politics as they intersect with stardom and celebrity may be observed in the range of articles published in the first six years of the journal *Celebrity Studies*, which published its inaugural issue in 2010: Sean Redmond's 'Avatar Obama in the Age of Liquid Celebrity' (2010), Anita Brady's '"This is Why Mainstream America Votes Against Gays, Adam Lambert": Contemporary Outness and Gay Celebrity' (2011), Deborah Jermyn's '"Get a Life, Ladies. Your Old One is Not Coming Back": Ageing, Ageism and the Lifespan of Female Celebrity' (2012), and Ruth A. Deller's 'Star Image, Celebrity Reality Television and the Fame Cycle' (2016). These studies, and indeed the journal itself, not only serve to exemplify the increasingly interdisciplinary nature of the field, but also the continued broadening of the field to encompass stardom as manifested in the film industry, and questions of stardom and celebrity as perpetuated through other media including television and, more recently, social media.

Within this burgeoning interest in the study of stardom and celebrity in the second half of the twentieth century and the first decades of the twenty-first century, another significant approach has been to investigate the history of ideas of stardom and celebrity prior to the development of mass market entertainment industries in the twentieth century. These studies provide a broader historical contextual positioning of the study of stardom and celebrity. Inglis, in his *A Short History of Celebrity*, aligns the development of the social processes of fame, celebrity and stardom with the acceleration of the development of modernity from the mid-eighteenth century. 'The business of renown and celebrity has been in the making for two and a half centuries. It was not thought up by the hellhounds of publicity a decade ago' (Inglis, 2010, p. 3). Historical studies such as Inglis' provide a greater context for the theorising of stardom that had originally assumed a focus on the stars of the film industry alone.

Despite its origins within film studies in the second half of the twentieth century, the broadening of the study of the processes of stardom and celebrity, and the increasingly interdisciplinary nature of these studies, have also observed an increase in the analysis of the role of stardom within the production and reception of popular music. In considering issues of stardom within the popular music industry, many of the same questions of star construction and reception apply, though particulars of the mechanics of the music industry necessarily shape perspectives on these issues. Similarly, many questions of identity as negotiated through processes of stardom remain current when examining the reception of the stars of popular music.

Identifying the point at which stardom became a key aspect of the popular music industry is difficult. However, as a star whose public persona drew on his professional activities as both a popular musician and screen actor during the 1940s and 1950s, Frank Sinatra's stardom was not only an early example of stardom within the postwar US popular music industry, but also an example of the potential overlap in the nature of stardom within both the film and music industries. Karen McNally argues that, while 'Sinatra is best known and most respected as a singer', the intertextual nature of Sinatra's star image derives from the combination of his renown as a musician and his presentation of character within films. 'Sinatra's film identity began as this overt combination of character and star image—an image that predates cinematic connections, reinforcing the importance of extrafilmic image construction' (McNally, 2008, p. 7). Sinatra's multifaceted career highlights the potential for stardom within the popular music industry to be augmented through other professional activities.

The emergence of rock-and-roll in the 1950s and the prominence of artists such as Chuck Berry and Elvis Presley have been identified by David R. Shumway as signifying the emergence of a rock stardom, arguing 'there was no rock and roll before there were rock stars' (2007, p. 530). Shumway further says 'the full-blown phenomenon of rock stardom did not develop until the Beatles and Rolling Stones were able to use Elvis' example as a conception of a career path' (p. 530). This is corroborated by other historical accounts and studies of star production, such as Martin Cloonan's 'The Production of English Rock and Roll Stardom in the 1950s' (2009) and Ian Inglis' 'Ideology, Trajectory and Stardom: Elvis Presley and the Beatles' (1996).

Successful rock-and-roll artists of the 1950s and 1960s set a precedent for the reception of stars in the later twentieth century. Michael Jackson exemplifies this, reaching the pinnacle of popular music stardom, first as a child star in the 1970s with Motown's The Jackson Five and later as a solo pop artist. Jacqueline Warwick (2012) identified his 'massive appeal, historical significance, celebrity status and artistic accomplishments' (p. 241) as elements of his stardom and cited 'discomfort with his career as a child star' (p. 242) as affecting the surprising lack of critical and scholarly attention. Interestingly, this understanding of stardom rejects the economic component of relative commercial success, instead focusing on artistic achievement.

Yet, monetary success is one significant way in which music stardom is commonly measured. In a key work on the economics of stars in the areas of sport and the arts, Moshe Adler (2006, p. 897) interpreted 'super stars' as those having 'considerable prominence and success in their field and whose earnings as a result are significantly greater than the earnings of their competitors'. Adler argues that 'super stardom' is not commensurate with talent, as has been previously argued by Sherwin Rosen (1981). Rather, stardom is attributable to consumers and their need to consume the same art as others to acquire 'consumption capital':

> Appreciation increases with knowledge. But how does one know about music? By listening to it, and by discussing it with other persons who know about it. In this learning process lies the key to the phenomenon of stars. (Adler, 1985, p. 208)

Viewed in this way, stardom may be construed as a measurement of popularity by quantity of consumers, in both the acquisition of recordings and concert attendance, and is not necessarily an indicator of musical ability or talent.

Personal identification with stars on the part of the consumer is a significant aspect of the process of star consumption and reception. In popular music, this process is mediated by the music and the meanings consumers interpret in the music. Often, consumers attempt to interpret the music and lyrics of a star persona by looking for connections between the music and details of the personal lives of the individual artist and themselves. Thus, the meaning received works in conjunction with an individual's identification with a star's publicly presented persona to strengthen the perceived connection between the consumer and the star. Through an analysis of print biographies of popular musicians,

Toynbee (2000) noted an assumption that the meaning of the music could be found in the lives of its makers. His argument is that 'musicians are exemplary agents who make a difference, in the shape of different songs, sounds and styles' (2000, p. x). The music, in this context, is primary; its production 'carries the promise of transcendence of the ordinary' (2000, p. x), and functions as a banner under which ordinary people can create community, with the musicians as 'representatives mandated by "their" people' (2000, p. x). Meaning, then, is the subject of negotiation between the producers and audience.

Similarly, Roy Shuker (2012) has discussed stardom in popular music as a consequence of the interaction between artistic creativity and audience reception:

> Stardom in popular music, as in other forms of popular culture, is as much about illusion and appeal to the fantasies of the audience, as it is about talent and creativity. Stars function as mythic constructs, playing a key role in their fans ability to construct meaning out of everyday life. Such stars must also be seen as economic entities, a unique commodity form which is both a labour process and product, effectively brands who mobilize audiences and promote the products of the music industry. (pp. 318–319).

Shuker (2012, p. 319) argues that the study of stardom in popular music has been limited and has generally produced a discourse that revealed 'how stardom has become a construct with a number of dimensions: the economic, the cultural and the aesthetic or creative'. Importantly, Shuker argues that fascination with the stars of popular music cannot be simply explained in terms of the political economy. Values such as authenticity, which are invested in individual musicians, create and maintain the notion of the star through the fanatic ritual of adoration and transcendence. Many contemporary stars are now frequently considered auteurs, carefully maintaining control over their public profile. Recent developments in the field of celebrity studies have involved a redefinition of the public/private boundary with an emphasis on the private life rather than the career becoming prominent (Shuker, 2012, p. 320).

While there might be many biographies of, or extensive literature on, a popular musician or band written by both journalists and academics, Shuker is one of only a handful of scholars who have considered the connections between popular music, stars and stardom more broadly. The interrelationship of ritual, pleasure and economics in popular music continues to create audiences, he declares, fuelling 'individual fantasy … and [the creation of] musical icons and cultural myths' (2016, p. vii). The musical icons, the stars, cultural myths and the stardom are inherent in popular music and vital to its existence.

Shuker's recent edition of *Understanding Popular Music Culture* devotes a chapter to auteurs and stars (2016, pp. 59–80) and draws on more recent examples of artists as stars than those used in the previous editions, including Lady Gaga, Taylor Swift and Lorde. As in earlier editions, Shuker's chapter continues to rely on highlighting individual career profiles that illustrate 'the interaction of musical authorship with genres, the music industry, fans and audiences, and history' (2016, p. 7), although displaying a shift to equal gender and more contemporary representation. There is a fine distinction between popular music stardom and auteur status; the latter signifying the reception of an artist as being genuinely creative, and one who explores and extends the dimensions of their art form. The attribution of auteur status to an artist rests on 'necessarily ambiguous' (Holmes, 2004, p. 154) notions of authenticity, while stars 'function as mythic constructs' that operate beyond the production of a substantial body of work, and reinterpret or reaffirm popular music styles and genres.

This authenticity discourse concerns the significance of popular musicians received by their audiences as 'authentic', bringing questions of star construction into sharper relief. Issues of auteurship, performance and the presentation of the self have long driven discussions, among fans and critics alike, regarding what distinguishes those considered 'authentic' artists from those perceived as industry constructions.[1] The attribution of star status is often reserved within discourses on popular music for artists considered to fulfil one or more of the criteria of authenticity as a popular music artist. P. David Marshall's chapter, 'The Meanings of the Popular Music Celebrity: The Construction of Distinctive Authenticity', part of his larger study *Celebrity and Power: Fame in Contemporary Culture* (1997), examines these issues in relation to the operation of stardom within the popular music industry. This intersection between pop/rock stardom and attributions of authenticity highlights connections between the star status achieved by artists and canon formation in rock and pop music.

---

1   For further discussion of debates concerning authenticity in popular music studies, see Allan F. Moore (2002) and Keir Keightley (2001).

From the expansion of the record industry simultaneous to the advent of rock-and-roll, numerous popular musicians have been assimilated into a rock/pop canon, similar in construction to canons of repertoire and composers in Western art music.[2] Since the establishment of the rock canon, many African-American jazz and blues musicians have been admitted, in belated recognition of contribution of these artists to the musical and aesthetic foundation of rock and pop music. Stardom, in conjunction with endurance, is one factor that informs canonisation. The ability for the work of a popular music artist to be strongly received not simply at the time, but over time, is integral to its potential canonisation. However, as Carys Wyn Jones noted, the construction of a rock canon involves many records and artists widely received as non-rock music. Wyn Jones argues that some records are assimilated into the rock canon not necessarily because they are rock albums, but because they display rock values, 'albeit ones inherited from the high arts' (2008, p. 2). Cleveland's Rock & Roll Hall of Fame and Museum[3] is a good example of the ascription of rock values to artists and works of other genres. Inductees include rap stars Tupac Shakur and NWA, pop stars ABBA and the Bee Gees, and funk stars Sly and the Family Stone and Funkadelic. Inductions also include affiliates of rock performance such as electric guitar pioneers Leo Fender and Les Paul, and producers including Leonard Chess, Glyn Johns and Quincy Jones, suggesting that some associates and affiliates of canonised rock artists are received as equally important as the stars themselves.

Another significant aspect of the role of stardom in the process of canon formation is the posthumous canonisation of popular music artists. That the posthumous attainment of canonical status is more often attributed to stars of rock and hip-hop than those of pop music aligns with the critical reception of rock and hip-hop as valorising auteurship over the performance of the works of others. It is unsurprising, then, that the star status of such artists becomes heightened upon their death. More recently, as Catherine Strong and Barbara Lebrun noted in *Death and the Rock Star* (2015), there is a growing fascination with the ramifications of death in popular music, in terms of both commercial potential and reception. The authors themselves admit to a shared fascination with popular music

---

2   For a discussion on canon formation in Western art music, see Lydia Goehr (2007).
3   See rockhall.com/inductees for a full list of Rock & Roll Hall of Fame and Museum inductees.

stars that have committed suicide (Strong and Lebrun, 2015, p. 1). This is an innovative and insightful exploration of death in popular music, covering the gamut of popular music's most renowned deaths.

Indeed, the death of a star, or a declining star career, is often discussed using 'falling' or 'fallen' star metaphors. For example, the careers of former rock stars Gary Glitter and Ian Watkins, and pop star Gloria Trevi, all ended as a consequence of their convictions for serious crimes. In each of these cases, journalists routinely used 'fallen star' narratives to refer to the immediate drop in the cultural status of these artists, the inevitable result of such crimes.[4]

Within discourses of popular music and rock stardom, and the processes of pop/rock canonisation, women are often the hidden stars. Pop/rock historiography is largely written by men. Therefore, documented histories, critiques and interpretations of contributions made by female and non-binary identifying musicians to popular music are limited. Of note, then, is that in this edited collection, three biographical chapters that focus on women musicians are presented. In a counter narrative to the desire for stardom are Australian musicians Judy Jacques and Wendy Saddington, who shrugged off star status in the 1960s and 1970s to pursue creative paths independent of the popular music industry. While we now see a greater diversity of types of star and celebrity, 'whether with regard to TV, pop music, film, sport, or people working across different media forms' (Holmes, 2004, p. 151), a feminist critique will readily highlight that a male bias within the cultural industries continues. Conversely, Beyoncé has taken control of the 'holistic world' across her music, videos, concerts and media presence (Macrossan, Chapter 8). She has successfully constructed, managed and facilitated her connection with her audience through the production of musical outputs perceived to be unique and significant within the current congested popular music landscape. This suggests that the immediacy and global capture of contemporary technology and social media provide greater opportunities for popular musicians to establish an audience base and then to operate more independently of the major industry players.

---

4   In 2008, Reuters reported on Glitter's conviction for molestation. The article of 14 August began 'Fallen British rock star Gary Glitter …' (Binh, 2008). In December 2013, shortly after Lost Prophets lead singer Ian Watkins was convicted of multiple child sex offences, newspaper *Wales Online* published an article referring to Watkins as a 'fallen rock star'. In 2002, *The Sydney Morning Herald* journalist Richard Boudreaux referred to Gloria Trevi as a 'fallen rock star' following her return to Mexico from Brazil after being convicted of child sex offences.

The late twentieth century has witnessed the rise of music technology stars, in terms of designers, engineers and equipment. In *Sound City*, for example, Foo Fighters guitarist and documentary director Dave Grohl (2013) foregrounded the recording studio's Neve 8078 console and its designer, British electronics engineer Rupert Neve, as the 'stars' of the documentary, equal in status to the studio's recording artists and canonical recordings. This notion of what Bennett has called 'technological iconicity' (2012) is increasingly visible in discourses of technological stardom. Consider, for example, this definition of masterclasses for the 2017 convention of the Audio Engineering Society (AES, 2017):

> An AES Master Class is given by an expert recognized in the field; a well-known star with name recognition. There is one presenter per session. An example would be having Rupert Neve talk about console design; or Mr Marshall talk about guitar amplifier design. This can be thought of as a star discussing something that was famous, or a high-level tutorial, covering advanced applications. We hope to draw people into the convention to hear a star.[5]

The canonisation of popular music stars has, therefore, clearly extended far beyond artist, genre and recording.

Today, the notion of popular music stardom is manifested in its most instant, gratifying and exaggerated form in the television reality program. Su Holmes (2004, p. 147) recognised the ways in which programs including *Popstars* and *Pop Idol* 'place the entire notion of stardom at center stage'. Reality television shows, including *The Voice*, *X Factor* and programs based on other similar formats, project an aspirational notion of stardom as manufactured, potentially transformative and instantaneous. Central to these shows are the music industry power intermediaries, in some cases in conjunction with the voting public, who decide which of the performers project the necessary star aura, narrowing the competition until an eventual winner is selected. Unsurprisingly, many tensions exist surrounding these formats. The emphasis on singing and performing cover versions of well-known contemporary songs obscures understandings of stardom based on notions of auteurship and originality. Since the consolidation of rock stardom in the 1960s, perceptions of musicality and originality have been central to the attribution of auteur status to popular musicians and, therefore, to the shaping of rock and stars in the

---

5   See the proposal submission page of the Audio Engineering Society website: aes.org/events/session_proposals/ (page discontinued, accessed April 2017).

commercial music industry. Thus, overshadowing of these values within projections of popular music stardom presented in these reality television programs is often treated with suspicion. The manufactured aspect of 'overnight success' that such television shows convey also contradicts notions of the endurance of reception so intrinsic to pop/rock canonical values. Yet, these shows successfully achieve the mediation of the aesthetics of stardom via live performance and the pressures commensurate with performance to large audiences. To reveal these somewhat intangible aesthetics of stardom, Mark Duffett (2009) has explored the aura elicited by musicians in live performance. He noted an intangible 'symbolic economy' of cultural power surrounding the star and recognised how fans who 'talk about live concerts and meetings with stars adopt terms like "power", "energy," and "electricity" as their currency of discussion' (p. 41). Critically, he noted heckling by audience members as a symbolic gesture that not only shifts the power balance between performers and fans, but also disrupts the aura of stardom emanating from the stage. This significant interpretation of stardom underlines the importance of the intangible in the star construct—canonisation, economic and commercial success and/or talent do not of themselves make a star.

Therefore, in popular music studies, we see the notions of stars, stardom and celebrity manifest in myriad ways. While we do not seek to investigate all potential lines of inquiry within this collection, nor discuss all artists considered stars of popular music, the studies brought together in this volume illuminate some interesting perspectives that serve to contribute to the developing discourse on stardom in popular music. When first discussing a theme for the 2015 Conference of the Australia and New Zealand branch of the International Association for the Study of Popular Music (IASPM), a focus on stars and stardom within popular music emerged after it was realised that, surprisingly, such an investigation had not been previously attempted in either a regional or an international conference of IASPM. Stars and stardom, it seemed, were so intertwined with contemporary popular music that their alignment had almost been taken for granted. The theme of 'Popular Music, Stars and Stardom' proved a fruitful field for exploration, with scholars addressing the theme and its related subjects from a variety of perspectives. Biographical appraisals were prevalent, and various applications of astronomical metaphors, in both cultural commentary and academic discourse, illuminated many inquiries. Others provided a critical discourse of stardom in the popular music industry more broadly. Collectively, the presentations demonstrated that popular music, stars and stardom were subjects ripe for investigation. The chapters that follow derive from papers that were first delivered at the conference, and serve to demonstrate that there remains scope for continued analysis of questions of stardom as they relate to popular music, its production and its reception.

The aims of this book, therefore, are threefold. First, in assembling a collection of chapters dedicated to the study of stars and stardom, we hope to bring together an overview of current discourse in this important, yet varied field. Second, we aim to expand on understandings of stardom via seven key works, each of which approaches the topics of stars and stardom in popular music from original angles. Third, we aim to reveal understandings of stardom by focusing on areas usually hidden in mainstream cultural commentary. This collection, therefore, explores stardom with emphasis on gender (in chapters by Robin Ryan, Julie Rickwood and Phoebe Macrossan), race (in chapters by John Whiteoak and Vincent Perry), the understudied areas of stardom in songwriting (in a chapter by Clive Harrison) and in the confluence of popular music and opera (in a chapter by Eve Klein).

In 'Interstellar songwriting: What Propels a Song Beyond Escape Velocity?', Clive Harrison uses a galactic metaphor to investigate creativity in the songwriting domain. Here, Mihaly Csikszentmihalyi's systems model of creativity (1988) is used as a framework to examine the ways songwriters negotiate their own creativity in the context of the field. Harrison posits the notion of the 'Pro-c' or professional songwriter and how factors affecting their songwriting practice have the potential to move them to 'Big-c' or paradigm-shifting creativity. Harrison recognises 'discriminant pattern recognition, naturalistic intelligence, productivity, fruitful asynchrony, propulsion theory, risk, field switching, expert variation and selective retention, and the production of significant works' as influencing the creative process of songwriting to varying degrees. In his findings, Harrison notes the confluence of 'exceptional choices based on "intuition"' and applications of 'dogged persistence, determination, focus, application' and other attributes as traits of a songwriter's expert status. This innovative chapter's galactic metaphors elucidate the construction of stardom within a songwriter's creative process.

John Whiteoak shifts the discussion of stars and stardom to the pre-jazz age in 'A Good Black Music Story? Black American Stars in Australian Musical Entertainment Before "Jazz"'. Here, Whiteoak critically negotiates the topic by first acknowledging the work of Ronald Radano in the construction of 'good' black music stories and the influence of both black and white sources that inform them. He goes on to recognise how 'numerous African-American singers, dancers and instrumentalists performed in Australia before Australia's Jazz Age' and in focusing on this era, illuminates the hidden stars that underpinned the emergence and development of Australian Jazz. In an insightful account of turn-of-the-century Australian touring vaudeville, minstrelsy and early jazz, Whiteoak traces the impact of acts including Sheraden Corbyn's Original Georgia Minstrels, the Hicks-Sawyer Minstrels and Hugo's Colored Minstrels; the latter Whiteoak evaluates as ending 'a three-and-a-half-decade era in which African-American artists contributed directly to the shaping and content of popular music in Australia'. Finally, the contribution to Australian Jazz made by African-American star musicians is noted as a 'good black music story' deserved of its place in Australian music history.

This book makes a significant contribution to understandings of stars and stardom by revealing contributions made to popular music by understudied female artists. In 'You're Messin' Up My Mind: Why Judy Jacques Avoided the Path of the Pop Diva', Robin Ryan posits a case of 'stardom in flux' in the career of this overlooked Australian roots artist. In this critical biography, Ryan traces how Jacques negotiated a complex of stardoms during her career. First, Ryan recognises Jacques as a teenage jazz star and the formation of cult status surrounding her artistry. Moving into the 1960s, Ryan reveals Jacques' relationship with television and the commercial record industry and how her image adapted to the demands of mainstream media. Ryan notes the global reach of Jacques' stardom with the track 'You're Messin' Up My Mind' and its dissemination via Manchester's Northern Soul scene. The tension between Jacques' conformity to mainstream media stardom, and her own artistic integrity is discussed in insightful sections on free singing, autonomous and heritage stardom as Ryan concludes that Jacques' career was a negotiation between 'musical freedom and industry objectification'.

Providing another perspective on the Australian female artist and stardom, Julie Rickwood considers the legacy of the late underground rhythm-and-blues artist Wendy Saddington. In a revealing account of Saddington's career, Rickwood contextualises the performer's work in 1970s Australian popular music before exploring the influence of African-American rhythm-and-blues stars on Saddington's aesthetic. Posthumously, Saddington is posited as a pioneer, equal in artistic contribution to the Divinyls' Chrissy

Amphlett. Rickwood evaluates Saddington's musical legacy, as well as her nonconformist identity in an illuminating account of a star otherwise hidden in Australian music historiography. Finally, Rickwood notes aspects of memory, heritage and commemoration among Saddington's fans, as manifested in the 2015 exhibition 'Underground Icon', held at Canberra Museum and Gallery. Rickwood concludes by noting how Saddington has been described as 'mercurial', her early career 'meteoric', her later performances occurring 'once in a blue moon' and her spiritual path into Krishna Consciousness 'transcendent', thus, articulating a cultural understanding of Wendy Saddington as an underground star.

Continuing the theme of revealing hidden stars, Vincent Perry's chapter focuses on the critical, yet rarely illuminated 'behind the scenes' musicianship of an important backing group. In 'Unsung Heroes: Recreating the Ensemble Dynamic of Motown's Funk Brothers', Perry considers the prolific and accomplished musicianship of the musicians of Berry Gordy's Motown backing band and seeks to highlight the prominence of their individual musical flair in the construction of Hitsville USA's iconic sound. Perry considers the concealed nature of recording artist backing bands in the 1960s and the tensions between musician anonymity relative to star performativity. In an exploration of creative practice, Perry's work then applies the ensemble dynamic of the Funk Brothers to his own recording project Soul Sundays. This account of practice-led research recreates the environmental, instrumental and aesthetic components of a Motown project and evaluates interpersonal skills, the limitations of historical recording processes and unified performance as major factors on its success.

In a chapter on the clashing of worlds of stardom, Eve Klein considers both the musical synergies and critical tensions in a record conflating two stars of entirely different musical spheres. 'When Divas and Rock Stars Collide: Interpreting Freddie Mercury and Montserrat Caballé's *Barcelona*' posits Mercury's contribution as a natural extension of his fascination with opera. Klein first unpacks opera's location within popular culture: the presence of the operatic canon on record, the 'crossover' repertoire and operatic appropriations. She notes the consideration of the Mercury/Caballé duo as eccentric before analysing the similarities in musical style between Queen's 'Bohemian Rhapsody' and Mercury/Caballé's 'Barcelona'. Here, Klein notes 'the aesthetic tendency underpinning both releases is operatic pastiche woven through rock with heavily mediated, hyper-real music production devices'. In conclusion, Klein considers 'Barcelona' in the contexts of both opera and rock and evaluates the record's difficult reception due to the ways it 'antagonises multiple authenticity gaps between operatic and rock performance styles'. Ultimately, Klein's article is a fascinating insight into the middlebrow; the collision of rock and opera stars is not necessarily a successful one.

In a fitting conclusion to this collection, Phoebe Macrossan shines a spotlight on one of today's biggest pop stars. In 'Intimacy, Authenticity and "Worlding" in Beyoncé's Star Project', Macrossan interprets Beyoncé's success as less a narrative of stardom and more a 'star project'. Here, she illustrates the construction of Beyoncé's 'world' as one extending beyond visual imagery to incorporate both 'the active process of creating a world and the world itself'. Macrossan posits Beyoncé's recent album *Lemonade* as an example of the star's 'worlding'; the music, imagery and political ideology along with an epic 60-minute film clip encapsulate this contemporary star's conceptual approach to artistic endeavour. Macrossan uses concepts adapted from film theory to scaffold her discussion of Beyoncé's 'worlding' before using the critically acclaimed *Lemonade* as an example case study. Macrossan concludes that Beyoncé's 'negotiation of stardom is now a strategy of constructing, maintaining and occupying Beyoncé World', also noting the active participatory role played by Beyoncé's audience in the maintenance of her 'worlds'.

These chapters conceptualise the manifestation of stardom in popular music and in wider media. In doing so, they reveal hidden stars, illuminate fading stars, foreground shadowed stars and offer a breadth of analytical and contextual insight into this evolving discourse.

References

Adler, M. 1985. 'Stardom and Talent'. *American Economic Review* 75 (1): 208–212.

——. 2006. 'Stardom and Talent'. In *Handbook of the Economics of Art and Culture*, edited by V. A. Ginsburg and D. Throsby, 895–906. Amsterdam: North-Holland.

Audio Engineering Society. 2017. 'AES Convention Proposals: Workshops, Tutorials, Master Classes, Game Audio etc.' aes.org/events/session_proposals/ (page discontinued, accessed April 2017).

Bennett, S. 2012. 'Endless Analogue: Situating Vintage Technologies in the Contemporary Recording & Production Workplace'. *Journal on the Art of Record Production* 7.

Binh Minh, H. 2008. 'Vietnam to Free Gary Glitter This Month'. Reuters, 1 August. reuters.com/article/us-vietnam-glitter-idUSHAN 13338820080802 (accessed March 2017).

Boorstin, D. 1971. *The Image: A Guide to Pseudo-Events in America*. New York: Atheneum.

Boudreaux, R. 2002. 'Fallen Rock Star Flies Home to Face the Music in Sex Scandal'. *Sydney Morning Herald*, 23 December. smh.com.au/articles/2002/12/22/1040510964491.html (accessed March 2017).

Brady, A. 2011. '"This is Why Mainstream America Votes Against Gays, Adam Lambert": Contemporary Outness and Gay Celebrity'. *Celebrity Studies* 2 (3): 292–304. doi.org/10.1080/19392397.2011.609335

Cloonan, M. 2009. 'The Production of English Rock and Roll Stardom in the 1950s'. *Popular Music History* 4 (3): 271–287.

Csikszentmihalyi, M. 1988. 'Society, Culture, and Person: A Systems View of Creativity'. In *Conception of Giftedness*, edited by R. J. Sternberg and J. Davidson, 325–339. New York: Cambridge University Press.

Deller, R. A. 2016. 'Star Image, Celebrity Reality Television and the Fame Cycle'. *Celebrity Studies* 7 (3): 373–389. doi.org/10.1080/19392397.2015.1133313

Duffett, M. 2009. '"We Are Interrupted by Your Noise": Heckling and the Symbolic Economy of Popular Music Stardom'. *Popular Music and Society* 32 (1): 37–57. doi.org/10.1080/03007760802207734

Dyer, R. 1998. *Stars*. New edition, with a supplementary chapter and bibliography by Paul McDonald. London: British Film Institute. Original edition, 1979.

——. 2004. *Heavenly Bodies: Film Stars and Society*. 2nd ed. Abingdon: Routledge.

Geraghty, C. 2000. 'Re-examining Stardom: Questions of Texts, Bodies and Performance'. In *Reinventing Film Studies*, edited by C. Gledhill and L. Williams, 183–202. London: Arnold.

Gledhill, C (ed.). 1991. *Stardom: Industry of Desire*. London: Routledge. doi.org/10.4324/9780203400425

Goehr, L. 2007. *The Imaginary Museum of Musical Works: An Essay in the Philosophy of Music*. Oxford: Oxford University Press.

Grohl, D., J. A. Rota and J. Ramsay. 2013. *Sound City*. Roswell Films Ltd.

Holmes, S. 2004. '"Reality Goes Pop!": Reality TV, Popular Music and Narratives of Stardom in Pop Idol'. *Television and New Media* 5 (2): 147–172. doi.org/10.1177/1527476403255833

Inglis, F. 2010. *A Short History of Celebrity*. Princeton: Princeton University Press. doi.org/10.1515/9781400834396

Inglis, I. 1996. 'Ideology, Trajectory and Stardom: Elvis Presley and the Beatles'. *International Review of the Aesthetics and Sociology of Music* 27 (1): 53–78. doi.org/10.2307/3108371

Jermyn, D. 2012. '"Get a Life, Ladies. Your Old One is Not Coming Back": Ageing, Ageism and the Lifespan of Female Celebrity'. *Celebrity Studies* 3 (1): 1–12. doi.org/10.1080/19392397.2012.644708

Keightley, K. 2001. 'Reconsidering Rock'. In *The Cambridge Companion to Pop and Rock*, edited by S. Frith, W. Straw and J. Street, 109–142. Cambridge: Cambridge University Press. doi.org/10.1017/CCOL9780521553698.008

Marshall, P. D. 1997. *Celebrity and Power: Fame in Contemporary Culture*. Minneapolis: University of Minnesota Press.

McNally, K. 2008. *When Frankie Went to Hollywood: Frank Sinatra and American Male Identity*. Urbana: University of Illinois Press.

Moore, A. F. 2002. 'Authenticity as Authentication'. *Popular Music* 21 (2): 209–223. doi.org/10.1017/S0261143002002131

Orgeron, M. 2008. 'Media Celebrity in the Age of the Image'. In *The Oxford Handbook of Film and Media Studies*, edited by R. Kolker, 187–223. Oxford: Oxford University Press. doi.org/10.1093/oxfordhb/9780195175967.013.0007

Oxford English Dictionary Online. 2016. Oxford University Press. oed.com

Redmond, S. 2010. 'Avatar Obama in the Age of Liquid Celebrity'. *Celebrity Studies* 1 (1): 81–95. doi.org/10.1080/19392390903519081

Redmond, S. and S. Holmes. 2007. 'Introduction: What's in a Reader?' In *Stardom and Celebrity: A Reader*, edited by S. Redmond and S. Holmes, 1–12. London: SAGE. doi.org/10.4135/9781446269534.n1

Rhys, S. 2013. 'Ian Watkins: Standing by Him Could Help Heal "A Very Broken Family" Says Stepdad'. *Wales Online*, 19 December. walesonline.co.uk/news/wales-news/ian-watkins-standing-him-could-6429786 (accessed March 2017).

Rosen, S. 1981. 'The Economics of Superstars'. *American Economic Review* 71: 845–858.

Shuker, R. 2012. *Popular Music Culture: The Key Concepts*. Abingdon and New York: Routledge.

——. 2016. *Understanding Popular Music Culture*. London: Routledge.

Shumway, D. R. 2007. 'Authenticity: Modernity, Stardom, and Rock & Roll'. *Modernism/Modernity* 14 (3): 527–533. doi.org/10.1353/mod.2007.0076

Strong, C. and B. Lebrun. 2015. *Death and the Rock Star*. London: Routledge.

Toynbee, J. 2000. *Making Popular Music: Musicians, Creativity and Institutions*. London: Oxford University Press.

Turner, G. 2014. *Understanding Celebrity*. 2nd ed. London: SAGE. doi.org/10.4135/9781473957855

Turner, G., F. Bonner and P. D. Marshall. 2000. *Fame Games: The Production of Celebrity in Australia*. Cambridge: Cambridge University Press.

Warwick, J. 2012. '"You Can't Win, Child, but You Can't Get Out of the Game": Michael Jackson's Transition from Child Star to Superstar'. *Popular Music and Society* 35 (2): 241–249. doi.org/10.1080/03007766.2011.618052

Wyn Jones, C. 2008. *The Rock Canon: Canonical Values in the Reception of Rock*. Aldershot: Ashgate.

2
Interstellar Songwriting: What Propels a Song Beyond Escape Velocity?

Clive Harrison

Introduction

Within the broadest cultural realm, and through the varied creativity definitions and process models presented by scholars (Bastick, 1982; Csikszentmihalyi, 1997, p. 80; Cropley, in Kaufman and Beghetto, 2009; Rothenberg and Hausman, 1976, p. 14; Sawyer, 2006, p. 89; Wallas, 1926), songwriting resides as a small but influential sub-domain of popular culture. Kaufman and Beghetto (2009) proposed an expanded model of creative magnitude in which mini-c refers to creativity in children, little-c refers to everyday innovation, Pro-c refers to professional creative expertise and Big-C refers to eminent accomplishment of paradigm-shifting or domain-changing creativity (pp. 1–12). The research question can be expressed in the following terms: 'how can the professional (Pro-c) songwriter move from "planetary" creativity, to "interstellar" (paradigm-shifting) Big-C creativity?'. Rather than view the songwriting goal as a binary, such as exploration and process, or the presentation of an artistic product, it is suggested that it is a confluence of all three. That is, a willingness and enthusiasm for exploration, a fascination with process and a consciousness of the presentation of an artistic product.

From McIntyre's (2003, p. 228) synthesis of theorists Csikszentmihalyi, Bourdieu and Negus, the most valuable lessons in this discussion for the songwriter are the following perspectives:

- Simply writing songs is necessary but not sufficient.
- Distribution and access to the domain and the field are vital.
- We write songs having first absorbed the song culture of the time.
- We cannot avoid having been influenced in our songwriting decisions in a profound way.

Also significant is the notion that for a song to become part of the domain it must be deemed worthy by the filter of the music industry (Csikszentmihalyi's field), and that songwriters act within a songwriting system of creativity in which agency and structure are interdependent. Further, Becker's *Art Worlds* (1982) reminds us that within the song-recording world, engineers, producers and other creative agents contribute to the song outcome and its potential for inclusion in the domain.

To consistently deliver worthy song contributions to the songwriting domain as a field professional, the Pro-c songwriter(s) need to act within the systems model of creativity (Csikszentmihalyi, 1988; Feldman, Csikszentmihalyi and Gardner, 1994). That is, they must acquire an expert knowledge of the domain, create songs that are deemed creative (for simplicity, defined herein as novel, useful and nonobvious)[1] and have access to the field—the experts, intermediaries, gatekeepers, critics and audience in that society.

---

1   Over the past 25 years, researchers have attempted to fine-tune a definition of creativity through a range of terminologies. For example, Kaufman and Sternberg (2010) vouch for the inclusion of 'originality', and highlight 'novelty' and 'quality', where quality also implies 'good' or 'useful' (p. 467). Gardner (1993) adds 'solving problems' and 'defining new questions' as outcomes of creativity (p. 33), and (noting the inculcation of habitus as described by Bourdieu) McIntyre (2006) includes notions of 'antecedent conditions' and makes the distinction of adding to the knowledge. Boden (2012) includes the term 'surprising' (p. 12), Weisberg (1993) requires the production of 'goal-directed novelty' (p. 244) and Sawyer (2006) advocates 'appropriateness' in his sociocultural definition of the term (p. 9). In deference to the United States Patent Office, Dean Keith Simonton (2014) includes the terms 'original' and 'non-obvious', the implication being that the invention would not be considered obvious to someone who has 'ordinary skill in the art'.

Overview

For this discussion, songwriting will be viewed as a creative task with varying degrees of magnitude from mini-c, through little-c, then Pro-c and, finally, the Big-C creativity of exemplars. Located within the sociocultural, and subject to the interdependency of field and domain, the following factors identified as influencing the creative process are examined: discriminant pattern recognition, naturalistic intelligence, productivity, fruitful asynchrony, propulsion theory, risk, field switching, expert variation and selective retention, and the production of significant works. A new term, 'adeptus', is offered to describe the confluence of these factors. For songwriters, it is posited that focus should be directed to its acquisition, rather than to factors beyond their control (the opinions of a particular music critic, for example, or a fortuitous opportunity occurring).

Adeptus and its Acquisition

By acquiring the habitus (Bourdieu, 1983) of the songwriting domain—that is, knowledge of the practical skills, techniques, concepts and procedures necessary for creating appropriate lyric, melody, harmony, rhythm, texture and style—quality song artefacts are more likely to be consistently created. Directed practice and reflection on songwriting procedures over an extended period is also necessary to develop expertise as a songwriter (as is the case with instrumental practice). Knowledge of the songwriting symbol system—the language, terminology and notation of popular music—is not essential, but is certainly an advantage for controlling performance elements and degrees of player interpretation on the live stage and in the studio. By acquiring such knowledge, quality song artefacts are more likely to be consistently created. The specific nomenclature and language of songwriters is geographically and historically inconsistent, changing generationally with conversational speech. As a result, it behoves songwriters to establish a common and contemporary argot for use, discussion, interaction and education. For the contemporary songwriter, however, domain knowledge from formal tuition alone is insufficient.

Songwriters benefit from, and need to be cognisant of, the role of informal, self-directed education and the vital domain acquisition derived beyond the classroom: the tacit knowledge and expertise of the seasoned professional. When habitus (through deep domain immersion), tacit knowledge (Polanyi, 1966; Schön, 1983), intuition (nonlinear parallel processing of global multicategorised information) (Bastick, 1982) and the unique distinctions borne of discriminant pattern recognition (naturalistic capacity) (Gardner, 1999) are combined with recursive, directed practice and reflection over an extended period, the resultant expertise or 'adeptus' (Harrison, 2016a) is likely to move creativity from little-c to Pro-c.

Adept: expert, skilful, nimble-fingered, capable, polished, professional, masterful.

Adeptus: all the attributes of an expert or master. More precisely:

> The combined expertise and tacit acquired knowledge resulting from the confluence of habitus (through deep domain immersion), intuition (nonlinear parallel processing of global multi categorised information), the unique distinctions borne of discriminant pattern recognition (naturalistic capacity) and the application of recursive, directed practice and reflection over an extended time-period. (Harrison, 2016a, pp. 396–97)

To move beyond Pro-c into the realm of Big-C creativity (cognisant that this is an attribution given 'after-the-fact' by the field of experts), it is argued that facilitative factors include a fruitfully asynchronous perspective, the capacity to challenge or reject the current paradigm and a willingness to risk rejection. It is not asserted that these elements provide all that is necessary for Big-C creativity to occur, merely that they are necessary for exemplary songwriting.

Discriminant Pattern Recognition

It is posited that an exceptional capacity for discriminant pattern recognition—that is, recognising, identifying and responding to important stimuli from the songwriting domain—is correlated to the Big-C creativity of exemplars. The very best songwriters simply observe in greater detail and respond more accurately to the culture in which they work creatively. Their unique perspective, experience and adeptus (all the attributes of the expert or master) provide the skill required to make nuanced choices that are otherwise unavailable to the average songwriter. Highly desirable for the songwriter, then, would be a strong capacity for naturalistic intelligence (Gardner, 1999) in the sense of its relation to song evolution and species (Bennett, 2011, 2012; Perkins, in Boden, 1996, p. 126).

Naturalistic Intelligence

In his multiple intelligence (MI) theory, Gardner (1983) presents a useful tool for songwriting practitioners that is especially geared to redress some of the imbalance of the general intelligence– or 'g'-based education system favoured by Spearman (1987, pp. 201–292). His 'eight intelligences' view (Gardner, 1999) provides a useful construct for examining creativity, and specifically songwriting, within the cultural milieu.[2] Prior research in the field has not specifically addressed songwriting practice. However, recent research (Harrison, 2016a), has uncovered the following distinctions.

At various stages in the songwriting process, songwriters may use all eight MIs: musical-aural and linguistic-verbal skills; the logical-mathematical skills of chord theory; recording and composition; visual-spatial factors in the recording of the song artefact using architectural, aural and temporal space; bodily-kinesthetic instrumental and/or vocal performance skills; and well-developed interpersonal, intrapersonal and naturalistic capacities. The last three capacities are highly valued and more likely to be selected by the field for their ability to reflect, specifically and consistently, what is valued, novel and nonobvious to the audience. Curiously, on this researcher's first view of MI theory some years ago, the capacity for naturalistic intelligence, described in Darwinian/evolutionary terms (Gardner, 1999, p. 48), seemed remote and possibly irrelevant to songwriting research. However, it can now be perceived as highly valuable—reflecting the capacity of songwriters to correctly identify and reproduce accurate song 'species'. A Darwinesque survival of the fittest is at play (Bennett, 2012), where songs survive or become extinct based upon whether the 'field' accepts the song artefact as a worthy inclusion in the domain. For recursive artefact evaluation during the creative process, astute use of naturalistic skill is a powerful differentiator between moderate and outstanding songwriting outcomes.

---

2   It should be noted that multiple intelligence theory takes a cognitive view of creativity, and is based on the *individual* node *as situated* within the systems model (Csikszentmihalyi, 1988; Feldman, Csikszentmihalyi and Gardner, 1994) that includes two other nodes, *domain* and *field*.

Significantly, this form of naturalistic domain acquisition is not normally included in formal music education. Its development relies largely on self-directed, informal immersion in the subculture (Green, 2013), and is most often achieved in two ways: by prolific songwriting, testing those songs on audiences, observing reactions and writing new songs for subsequent testing; or, through studious directed listening to songs that have been already accepted into the domain as worthy by the field, observing what appears to work and considering potential generalities. Both require the songwriter to actively participate outside the confines of the studio or the classroom—in the field itself.

Songwriting based upon deep immersion in a specific song style tends to garner industry support. Embracing the forward incrementation proposed by Sternberg, Kaufman and Pretz (2002), when incremental (rather than radical) change is preferred in creative practices in which the field is content with the state of the domain, the field recognises the near-analogous nature of the song compared with its antecedents. Song artefacts whose lineage and style are clear, then, tend to be more popular in commercial markets than those that are not. Conversely, artefacts whose lineage and style are obscure are more popular in avant-garde and local markets, as described by Lena and Peterson (2008), than those whose target market is obvious. However, for Thistlethwayte (2015), a heightened awareness of song lineage and antecedents is common, but it is desirable to use those earlier works as inspiration for exploration, rather than merely copying. The experienced professional can deconstruct his or her works post-hoc, and recognise influences (Connors, 2015), but what is valued is the unaccountable and personal choices they have made based on their own adeptus.

Productivity

For Sawyer (2006, p. 131), the popular notion of the solitary creator working on a single masterpiece that will change the world is 'more of a myth than reality'. Domain-changing or significant creativity is more commonly the realm of the prolific, highly productive, persistent agent—the creator of multiple works whose dogged persistence bears fruit (Gardner, 1993, pp. 343–345). Inventors and creators whose work is judged to be truly significant over time have the highest overall lifetime output, be they inventors (Huber, 1998, pp. 58–72) or creators (Simonton,

1988a, 1988b). Sawyer (2006, p. 131) describes such a creative process as the productivity theory, arguing that 'the best way to have a good idea is to have a lot of ideas, and then just get rid of the bad ones'. This suggests that by creating multiple artefacts, inventors and creators maximise their chance for an artefact to be deemed novel, useful and nonobvious (i.e. creative). The implication for Pro-c songwriters is that the goal is not to attempt to produce a singular masterpiece; rather, it is to produce a body of songwriting works from which the field may potentially select one or more masterpieces.

A further distinction should be made regarding high productivity. While the production of truly significant works can be correlated with highly productive creators, Sawyer's notion does not insist that such truly significant works must also constitute domain-changing or paradigm-shifting works. They may simply be deemed significant—that is, the best version, product or idea in the domain, based upon the collective evaluation of the field. For the Pro-c creative songwriter who does not necessarily set out to change the domain, and whose works follow the forward incrementation of someone content with the state of the domain and has no need to shift it, such an attribution is entirely possible and available.

What then of the highly productive, expert Pro-c songwriter who contributes multiple significant works over a lifetime but falls short of the ideal of paradigm-shifting creativity? For example, some might argue that the songs of Grammy award-winning Swedish producer and expert songwriter Max Martin have not shifted the domain of mainstream pop per se. However, it would be hard to argue that he has not produced some significant works among his 54 top-10 hits and 19 US number ones. From the perspective of Sternberg, Kaufman and Pretz's (2001) propulsion theory, his writing style is more accepting of the current paradigm, rather than rejecting or challenging it. While Martin's Grammy tally approaches that of John Lennon, some may assert that Lennon was the more creative; although to address that debate one would have to delve into sociocultural notions of authenticity beyond the scope of this chapter. From this research perspective, Lennon was willing to challenge or reject aspects of the existing paradigm, whereas Martin seems to have been content to accept and extend it. So, the question becomes: what provides the necessary extra impetus or propulsive power to propel the songwriter beyond functional Pro-c songs to eminent, significant or domain-changing Big-C creativity?

Fruitful Asynchrony

Howard Gardner (1993, p. 353) describes the distinction between factors influencing those who become 'creative' beyond mere 'experts', as fruitful asynchrony—that is, the 'capacity to exploit, or profit from, an apparent misfit or lack of smooth connections within the triangle of creativity'. This 'triangle of creativity' refers to the individual, domain and field of Csikszentmihalyi's systems model of creativity (1988). Applied to songwriting, asynchrony occurs when a songwriter is in some way out-of-step with the song culture of the day. That asynchrony becomes fruitful when it leads to the type of song that shifts the paradigm of the prevailing songwriting landscape, the realm of the Big-C creative songwriter. Those asynchronously fruitful songs can be described in terms of differently conceived creative propulsions.

Propulsion Theory

While a proliferation of songs, adequate expertise, creativity and access to the field might push the songwriter to a Pro-c level, creating songs that change the domain or shift the paradigm requires some additional (or alternative) skills. To actively change or shift the existing culture, it would be helpful at first to have perceived a need for change, or to be dissatisfied in some way with its current state. To that end, a perspective that is slightly different or fruitfully asynchronous with other songwriters would be desirable, along with an attendant willingness to create songs that challenge the current paradigms and potentially risk failure, or rejection. If each song is considered a creative propulsion, three types of new song paradigms are created: those that accept or extend the paradigm, those that reject or replace the current paradigm, and those that integrate or synthesise song styles. Further, eight types of creative propulsion are defined: replication, redefinition, forward incrementation, advance forward incrementation (that accept and/or extend), redirection, reconstruction, reinitiation (that reject or challenge) and synthesis (that integrates).

Risk

Most common among propulsions in the songwriting realm is forward incrementation, where the songwriter attempts to propel forward the new style with another song artefact with similar forward momentum of style. The 'riskier' approach of attempting to reject or replace the current paradigm might lead to songs more likely to change the paradigm, but may be avoided by a songwriter whose desired outcome is cultural acceptance, rather than cultural notoriety or change. For the Pro-c songwriter who is averse to risk-taking (less enthusiastic about exploration) in their professional creative work, asynchronous song possibilities may be difficult or present as undesirable choices. However, Pro-c songwriters who see the exploratory aspects of songwriting as desirable and a welcome challenge rather than a risky constraint may find themselves moving into the realm of domain-changing and paradigm-shifting song artefacts. An inexperienced songwriter could blindly experiment with all sorts of ill-informed, wild song explorations searching for asynchronous iterations that might prove fruitful, but the expert, with the adeptus to make astute variations, is far more likely to discover those divergent, remotely analogous possibilities that will bear fruit. One factor contributing to the capacity to identify remotely analogous, rather than near-analogous song possibilities, is when creativity-supporting skills are transferred from other disciplines, as is sometimes the case with field-switchers.

Field Switching

Following Sawyer's (2006, p. 115) argument that, 'creative combinations often result when people switch fields', it is suggested that cross-disciplinary skills can provide a useful source of fruitful asynchrony that opens remotely analogical possibilities for the creative agent (Harrison, 2016b). When the expert is able to transfer expertise from a different field, their unique perspective may identify paradigms they feel warrant challenging or rejecting. If a polymath (with expertise across two different fields of endeavour) manages to transfer domain-specific or domain-general skills across disciplines, the resultant creative products or propulsions are likely to be different. In terms of propulsion theory, these redirections, reconstructions, re-initiations or syntheses move away from where we are now. Therefore, skills possessed across unrelated disciplines may precipitate more divergent, remote-analogical solutions than those convergent solutions implied by closely related, domain-specific transfers. Field switching may be a factor that stimulates the creative person to explore propulsions that move away from where we are now, by introducing the type of fruitfully asynchronous, remotely analogous ideas that (if accepted by the field as worthy) tend to shift the paradigm (Harrison, 2016b).

Expert Variation and Selective Retention

It is suggested here that the capacity to be creative (that is, to come up with valuable, useful and nonobvious solutions) is available to anyone. Additionally, 'highly creative' people simply direct their attention towards remote-analogies more freely and successfully than 'less creative' people, who, for one reason or another, seek near-analogies as a matter of habit. A willingness to test, explore and embrace blind variation and selective retention (BVSR) (Campbell, 1960) is implied, where song possibilities include trial and error, randomised choices, unlikely solutions to songwriting 'problems' and risk-taking. However, the songwriter who possesses outstanding adeptus—expertise, tacit knowing, discriminant pattern recognition and habitus—is capable of informed trial and error, nuanced choice-making, well-advised solutions and measured risk-taking, significantly more than the novice or moderately equipped songwriter. Following Weisberg, who proposes a 'continuum between expert-based creativity and BVSR, with the important dimension being the depth of knowledge that the individual brings to the situation' (as summarised in Hass and Weisberg, 2015, p. 471), it follows that a highly skilled, deeply immersed songwriter might apply his or her unique adeptus as a form of 'expert' variation and selective retention (EVSR), a form of discriminant pattern recognition unavailable to lesser songwriters. From this informed EVSR perspective, solution-seeking is much more likely to be successful, resulting in more song candidates for potential acceptance by the field as 'significant' works rather than the random choices of a novice whose variations are 'blind'.

Significant Works

Sawyer (2006, p. 131) has identified that truly significant works tend to come from highly productive creators, but it is posited here that the distinction should be made that not all truly significant works are necessarily domain changing or paradigm shifting. Some may be simply the stand-out version, product or idea in that domain at the time. Until the field has cast its vote, we won't know which works are going to change the domain, and that may take years, decades or even centuries. Describing creativity that is 'new in history', Boden (1991, p. 269) states, 'what we identify as "H-creative" depends to a large extent on historical accident and social fashion'. This situation raises the songwriting question as to whether the attempt to create 'significant works' necessarily includes the requirement to change the domain or shift the paradigm.

Further, the question 'how can the songwriter move from (Pro-c) creativity, to (domain-changing) Big-C creativity?' is revealed to be misleading. It implies that the goal of the songwriter should be to change the domain, despite it having been shown that Big-C creativity is an attribution by the field, after the fact, as described by Sawyer (2006, p. 124): 'a creation's ultimate social importance can't be predicted from the mental processes involved; it results from a social process'. We can view it simply as a domain-changing iteration of Pro-c creativity. Thus, it is posited that the following distinction describes more accurately the songwriting continuum of 'greatness'. Within the broad description of Pro-c songwriting exists two forms of exemplar creativities: Big-C creativity includes all significant or eminent creativities whatever the style of creative propulsion, while a new term, 'Alt-C' creativity, includes 'alternative' creative propulsions that have been observed by the field to shift the paradigm or change the domain.

Conclusions

The confluent application of a songwriting methodology that embraces the systems model of creativity (Csikszentmihalyi, 1988), maximises the capacities of available MI (Gardner, 1983) and exploits creative propulsions acceptable to the field (Sternberg et al., 2002) is likely to be highly productive. Further, it is desirable to acquire a high level of expertise, allowing distinctions to be made that others would miss, or fail to recognise, as significant. These creators will make exceptional choices based on 'intuition' (i.e. 'feelings of warmth') (Nickerson, in Sternberg, 1999) as to the solutions most likely to produce novel and useful variations within the domain. They will apply the dogged persistence, determination, focus, application and other attributes described as qualities of the creative personality (Boden, 1996; Csikszentmihalyi and Csikszentmihalyi,

1991; Gardner, 1993) to arrive at the necessary adeptus of the expert or master. Supporting Boden's (1996) view of creativity, where H (historical) creativity is a subset of P (personal) creativity, it is posited that both Big-C and Alt-C creative songwriting can be considered subsets of Pro-c creativity (Harrison, 2016b)—the former representing significant song artefacts that accept or extend the paradigm (incrementally moving it forward), and the latter representing significant song artefacts that reject or challenge it (shifting the paradigm). The question as to 'what factors move the songwriter along the continuum from Pro-c creativity into the realm of Big-C creativity' no longer necessarily implies a hierarchy in which the highest goal of the songwriter should be to change the domain, and that Big-C is somehow greater than excellent Pro-c creativity. Rather, Big-C (and Alt-C) creativity can be considered significant iterations of Pro-c songwriting craft.

To move from planetary to interstellar songwriting, six contributory facilities have been identified. The first three precipitate the shift from Pro-c to Big-C creativity. Discriminant pattern recognition is the facility, in an evolutionary sense, to recognise similar species across domains and possess the adequate powers of differentiation, observation and evaluation to make informed distinctions that others cannot see (EVSR). Metacognition, Big-C creativity, requires a capacity for higher-order thinking skills that include analysis, evaluation and creation, and the resources (including time) to test for validity and reliability. Finally, productivity involves creating multiple artefacts to maximise the chances that one or more will be deemed novel and useful (i.e. creative).

Three further contributory facilities specifically direct creative outputs towards domain-changing or paradigm-shifting Alt-C creativity. Fruitful asynchrony is an asynchronous perspective that challenges the current paradigms. To be Alt-C creative, one would need to make distinctions differently to others in the domain to be able to create differently. Field-switching—expertise in multiple disciplines—is a fruitfully asynchronous factor that stimulates the creative person to explore propulsions that move away from the current position of the field. Field-switchers are more likely to make distinctions that other, less expert, less interdisciplined people cannot. Finally, risk is a willingness to explore possibilities without fear of failure. A successful Pro-c songwriter might be simply unwilling to take paradigm-challenging risks, and seek instead to create significant works that do not change the domain.

The idiosyncratic depth perspective and adeptus of the significant, interstellar Big-C songwriter utilises a capacity to observe and apply nuances of style, technique and habitus unnoticed or missed completely by the lesser songwriter. The very best songwriters, it would seem, simply listen better, notice differently and document their unique perspectives in song based on higher levels of adeptus.

References

Bastick, T. 1982. *Intuition: How We Think and Act.* Hoboken: John Wiley & Sons.

Becker, H. 1982. *Art Worlds.* Berkeley: University of California Press.

Bennett, J. 2011. 'Collaborative Songwriting – The Ontology of Negotiated Creativity in Popular Music Studio Practice'. *Journal on the Art of Record Production* 5. arpjournal.com/collaborative-songwriting-—-the-ontology-of-negotiated-creativity-in-popular-music-studio-practice/ (accessed 10 May 2018).

———. 2012. 'The Song Remains the Same—Why?' *Total Guitar*, June, 228. joebennett.net/2013/02/11/the-song-remains-the-same-why-from-total-guitar-magazine/ (accessed 10 May 2018).

Boden, M. 1991. *The Creative Mind: Myths & Mechanisms.* New York: Basic Books.

———. 1996. *Dimensions of Creativity.* Cambridge: MIT Press.

———. 2012. *Creativity and Art: Three Roads to Surprise.* Oxford: Oxford University Press.

Bourdieu, P. 1983. *The Field of Cultural Production: Essays on Art and Literature.* New York: Columbia University Press.

Campbell, D. T. 1960. 'Blind Variation and Selective Retentions in Creative Thought as in Other Knowledge Processes'. *Psychological Review* 67 (6): 380. doi.org/10.1037/h0040373

Connors, G. 2015. Interview by author. Mackay, QLD. 28 August.

Csikszentmihalyi, M. 1988. 'Society, Culture, and Person: A Systems View of Creativity'. In *Conception of Giftedness*, edited by R. J. Sternberg and J. Davidson, 25–339. New York: Cambridge University Press.

———. 1997. *Finding Flow: The Psychology of Engagement with Everyday Life*. New York: Basic Books.

Csikszentmihalyi, M. and I. S. Csikszentmihalyi. 1991. *Flow: The Psychology of Optimal Experience*, Vol. 41. New York: Harper Perennial.

Feldman, D. H., M. Csikszentmihalyi and H. Gardner. 1994. *Changing the World: A Framework for the Study of Creativity*. Westport: Praeger.

Gardner, H. 1983. *Frames of Mind—The Theory of Multiple Intelligences*. New York: Basic Books.

———. 1993. *Creating Minds: An Anatomy of Creativity as Seen Through the Lives of Freud, Einstein, Picasso, Stravinsky, Eliot, Graham, and Gandhi*. New York: Basic Books.

———. 1999. *Intelligence Reframed: Multiple Intelligences for the 21st Century*. New York: Basic Books.

Green, P. L. 2013. *How Popular Musicians Learn: A Way Ahead for Music Education*. Farnham: Ashgate Publishing.

Harrison, C. M. 2016a. 'A Songwriter's Journey from Little-c to Pro-C Creativity: An Applied Analytical Autoethnography'. PhD thesis, University of Newcastle, Newcastle, NSW.

———. 2016b. 'Bebop on the Hockey Pitch: Cross-Disciplinary Creativity and Skills Transfer'. *Performance Science* 7: 123. doi.org/10.3389/fpsyg.2016.00123

Hass, R. W. and R. W. Weisberg. 2015. 'Revisiting the 10-Year Rule for Composers. From the Great American Songbook: On the Validity of Two Measures of Creative Production'. *Psychology of Aesthetics, Creativity, and the Arts* 9 (4): 471–479. doi.org/10.1037/aca0000021

Huber, J. 1998. 'Invention and Inventivity as a Special Kind of Creativity, With Implications for General Creativity'. *Journal of Creative Behavior* 32 (1): 58–72. doi.org/10.1002/j.2162-6057.1998.tb00806.x

Kaufman, J. C. and R. A. Beghetto. 2009. 'Beyond Big and Little: The Four-c Model of Creativity'. *Review of General Psychology* 13 (1): 1–12. doi.org/10.1037/a0013688

Kaufman, J. C. and R. J. Sternberg. 2010. *The Cambridge Handbook of Creativity*. Cambridge: Cambridge University Press. doi.org/10.1017/CBO9780511763205

Lena, J. C. and R. A. Peterson. 2008. 'Classification as Culture: Types and Trajectories of Music Genres'. *American Sociological Review* 73 (5): 697–718. doi.org/10.1177/000312240807300501

McIntyre, P. 2003. 'Creativity and Cultural Production: A Study of Contemporary Western Popular Music Songwriting'. PhD thesis, Macquarie University, Sydney, Australia.

——. 2006. 'Paul McCartney and the Creation of "Yesterday": The Systems Model in Operation'. *Popular Music* 25 (2): 201–219. doi.org/10.1017/S0261143006000936

Polanyi, M. 1966. *The Tacit Dimension*. Chicago: University of Chicago Press.

Rothenberg, A. and C. Hausman. 1976. *The Creativity Question*. Durham: Duke University Press.

Sawyer, R. K. 2006. *Explaining Creativity: The Science of Human Innovation*. Oxford: Oxford University Press.

Schön, D. 1983. *The Reflective Practitioner: How Professionals Think in Action*. New York: Basic Books.

Simonton, D. K. 1988a. 'Creativity, Leadership, and Chance'. In *The Nature of Creativity: Contemporary Psychological Perspectives*, edited by R. J. Sternberg, 386–426. New York: Cambridge University Press.

——. 1988b. *Scientific Genius: A Psychology of Science*. Cambridge: Cambridge University Press.

——. 2014. 'Thomas Edison's Creative Career: Multilayered Trajectory of Trials, Errors, Failures, and Triumphs'. *Psychology of Aesthetics, Creativity, and the Arts* 9 (1): 2–14. doi.org/10.1037/a0037722

Spearman, C. 1987. 'The Proof and Measurement of Association between Two Things' (originally published 1904). *The American Journal of Psychology* 100 (3–4): 441–471. doi.org/10.2307/1422689

Sternberg, R. J. (ed.). 1999. *Handbook of Creativity*. Cambridge: Cambridge University Press.

Sternberg, R. J., J. C. Kaufman and J. E. Pretz. 2001. 'The Propulsion Model of Creative Contributions Applied to the Arts and Letters'. *The Journal of Creative Behavior* 35 (2): 75–101. doi.org/10.1002/j.2162-6057.2001.tb01223.x

———. 2002. *The Creativity Conundrum: A Propulsion Model of Kinds of Creative Contributions*. London: Routledge.

Thistlethwayte, R. 2015. Interview by author. Redfern, NSW. 27 April.

Wallas, M. G. 1926. *The Art of Thought*. London: C. A. Watts.

Weisberg, R. W. 1993. *Creativity: Beyond the Myth of Genius*. London: W. H. Freeman & Company.

3
A Good Black Music Story? Black American Stars in Australian Musical Entertainment Before 'Jazz'

John Whiteoak

Figure 3.1: Charles B. Hicks' Original Georgia Minstrels, 1885
Source: Australian Variety Theatre Archive: Popular Culture Entertainment: 1850–1930, ozvta.com/troupes-g-l/.

> History once stated that thick-lipped musicians were no good on brass instruments, especially the cornet. Well, that theory was killed when these coloured stars got on the job. (*Critic*, 1917)

A major problem in jazz-related research and writing has always been the use of terms like 'black music' or 'jazz' as what would be classed as 'master signifiers' according to the widely influential theories of psychoanalyst and theorist Jacques Lacan. Master signifiers are words like 'appropriate', which are used as 'placeholders' for things we do not fully understand or for which we lack satisfactory definitions. Lacan's theory refers to three categories of meaning associated with words: 'the symbolic' (what is signified), 'the imaginary' (what is imagined) and 'the real'.[1] The theory suggests that 'the real' can never be precisely known because of its integral interrelationship to what is both imagined and signified by a word.[2] Lacan's theories are controversial, sometimes contradictory and often misinterpreted, and were conceived specifically for psychoanalysis. Yet the simple notion or truism inherent in his notion of the master signifier—that particular words are used as placeholders for meanings that actually fall somewhere between what is signified and what is imagined by that word—can also be usefully applied to a relatively non-theoretical historical musicological analysis such as that presented below.

In *Lying Up a Nation: Race and Black Music*, ethnomusicologist and black music theorist Ronald Radano (2003) views the term 'black music' as a placeholder, but he uses 'lying' in the positive sense of black music being a 'good story' or good myth. Along with exhaustive critique of theoretical debate concerning black music, Radano (2003, p. 33) examines, through numerous early primary sources, the extent to which this 'good story' was constructed and essentialised by early white American commentators and their writings and representations (such as the blackface minstrel show) in 'white-over-black narration'. He proposes an alternative story based on a deep critique of the sources that have shaped the 'good black music story'. This story would be less of a caricature than, say, the controversial 2001 Ken Burns documentary *Jazz* (Pond, 2003, pp. 11–45): more nuanced, complex, interracial and all the more convincing, richer and dignifying for seeking 'musical truths among the gossamer of tall tales' (Radano, 2003, p. 42). It would be grounded in the understanding that early black

---

1 For an accessible overview of Lacan's psychoanalytic theory, see Bailly (2009).
2 The 'master signifier' analogy was inspired by a paper presented by composer and semiotics/music theorist Thomas Reiner (2015). See also Bailly (2009, pp. 61–64).

music history is not fully knowable in the same sense that Lacan's 'the real' is not fully knowable, but 'nonetheless voices a truth about life and nation' (Radano, 2003, p. 25). This study does not critique or apply Radano's many-stranded analyses and theories about the US's good black music story. Instead, it asks whether pre-jazz Australia could possibly be a part of this story, given that numerous African-American singers, dancers and instrumentalists performed in Australia before Australia's Jazz Age (c. 1918–28). It focuses on an especially important aspect of this question, primarily from a basic musicological perspective.[3] Given that the term 'jazz' was meaningless to the Australian public before the earliest overseas reports in late 1917, is it possible that the band and orchestra music associated with particular black minstrel shows that toured Australia before this time was an incipient form of black jazz?

'Early jazz' historiography has tended to emphasise the 'pure' folk roots of jazz and blues while turning a blind eye to the role of mainstream 'commercial' music-making of black band and orchestra musicians in early jazz development (Gennari, 2006, p. 121). The absence of early sound recordings of New Orleans jazz and vernacular blues greatly facilitated myth-making about the origins of jazz and blues. However, revision of the early black music story has in fact commenced with the work of scholars such as Lotz (1997), Abbott and Seroff (2002, 2007), Brooks (2004), Gushee (2005), Berresford (2010) and others. Berresford (2010, p. 7) points out that 'only recently has the pivotal role of touring minstrel shows and circus sideshow bands in the formative period of jazz and blues evolution been researched in any depth'. He further states that what these researchers are revealing:

> Flies in the face of the romantic notion of early jazzmen being gifted musical illiterates, pouring forth a stream of endless improvised melody, oblivious to the rules and conventions of 'proper' music. In reality, musicians groomed in the world of the tent show and the circus were those most in demand in other areas of musical activity. Orchestra leaders … valued highly the circus musicians' sight-reading and improvisational abilities, coupled with their ability to 'follow' a stage performer in their routine'. (pp. 28–29)

---

3   The chapter is significantly indebted to Waterhouse (1991) and the Australia-related content of Abbott and Seroff (2002).

Steven Lewis (2012) argues similarly in his thesis, '"Untamed Music": Early Jazz in Vaudeville', which 'challenge[s] previously held assumptions about … New Orleans as the sole birthplace of early jazz—and shed[s] light on jazz's place in the broader popular culture landscape of the early 20th century' (p. 10). He stresses the improvisatory nature of commercial black tent shows and vaudeville music making (Lewis, 2012, pp. 107–108). The famous so-called 'Father of the Blues', W. C. Handy (1970), complained about musicians who 'bowed to the authority of the printed note, unlike minstrel musicians who could "fake" and "sell it"' (p. 80). Readers of *Playing Ad Lib, Improvisatory Music in Australia: 1836–1970* (Whiteoak, 1999) will find many similarities to Berresford and Lewis' observations regarding the improvisatory nature of circus, variety, vaudeville and white and African-American minstrel-show music in Australia before jazz (Whiteoak, 1999, pp. 122–124, 150–152).

'Jazz' in Australia

Australian jazz history is widely considered to have commenced in June 1918 with the interstate tour of vaudeville act 'Australia's First Jazz Band'. Often cited as the first black jazz band to reach Australia, Sonny Clay's Plantation Orchestra arrived in 1928 as part of the Colored Idea Revue troupe, but was forced to depart following accusations of miscegenation and drugs (Johnson, 2010).

For the sake of later discussion of minstrel band and orchestra music, however, the term 'jazz' should be considered a placeholder for something that has meant, and continues to mean, many different things, according to when, where or who is defining it. For example, in jazz-age Australia, as elsewhere, jazz was used as a verb—'to jazz' or 'jazzing'—to mean embellishing and transforming popular music with African-American– inflected idioms to make it more rhythmic, colourful, entertaining, amusing, or (to use another master signifier) 'hot' (Whiteoak, 1999, pp. 168–230). Making popular music hot, or jazzing it, involved the improvisatory interpolation of idiomatic 'fills' or 'breaks', novelty sound effects and hot 'participatory discrepancies'—barely perceptible but expressive surface embellishments, ornamentations, timbrel variegations, over-blowing, rhythmic displacements and 'grooves', and other unscored alterations or creative 'noise-making' that essentially defy notation (Keil, 1994, p. 104). However, making popular music hot with idiomatic interpolations or alterations was called 'ragging' decades before the Jazz Age (Berlin, 1980, pp. 66–71) and had always been an essential aspect of blackface (white) minstrelsy and later black (African-American) minstrelsy in forms that reached Australia before the Jazz Age (Whiteoak, 1999, pp. 68–230; 2014, pp. 29–35).

In the 1994 article '"Jazzing" and Australia's First Jazz Band' (Whiteoak, 1994, pp. 279–295), I demonstrate that the observed jazzing or jazz improvisation of this ensemble was largely the ragging of ragtime repertoire. This ragging, or jazzing, was furthermore perceived to be related to the extroverted, unorthodox, noisy and highly comedic music of the 'old-time' minstrel-show orchestras: 'The band reminded one of the old-time N[egro] minstrel bands. For the most part the members made more noise than music—simply "jazzed" away for all they were worth' (*The Advertiser*, 1918).[4] The terms ragging and jazzing remained synonymous in Australia until the early 1920s. A key connection or continuity between the music, dance and acting of the black minstrel artists and ensembles discussed below and the earliest so-called 'jazz' or 'jazzing' in Australia lay very much in the notion of comic distortion or clowning, and in what was misconceived to be musical clowning.

Black Minstrelsy in Australia

The history of jazz-related music in Australia begins in 1838 when white colonial actor-dancer-musicians in burnt-cork make-up presented improvisatory 'Negro' music and dance acts like 'Jump Jim Crow' or 'Zip Coon' on the popular stage (Waterhouse, 1991, pp. 1–12; Whiteoak, 2014, pp. 29–34). These individual 'blackface' artists were followed a decade later by touring blackface (white) minstrel troupes with ear-playing minstrel 'orchestras' (typically) of banjo, fiddle, bones and tambourine, and featuring performance behaviour and improvisatory practices that anticipated those of ragtime and jazz, as documented in Whiteoak (1999, pp. 83–110; 2014, pp. 29–34).

---

4   See also Whiteoak (2014, p. 46).

- ear-playing
- head-arrangements
- percussion accompaniment, 'fill', 'breaks', solos and duets and 'imitations' on bones and tambourines
- polyrhythmic body percussion as 'patting juba dance accompaniment'
- syncopation, complex polyrhythm and improvisatory fills and variations on banjo
- 'talking banjo' (musical imitation of spoken replies)
- variations on fiddle, flutina and banjo
- musical burlesque and novelty noise
- improvisatory and extended vocal techniques
- collective improvisatory musical play
- incipient vocal and instrumental 'ragging'
- improvisatory dance.

Figure 3.2: Jazz-antecedent practices in minstrelsy
Source: Whiteoak (1999).

Black American artists were able to enter this field of entertainment after the 1861–65 Civil War, but, to be successful, they had to adopt and adapt the demeaning blackface stereotyping and comic distortion of themselves and their culture.[5] While white minstrels in burnt-cork make-up were respected for the cleverness of their parody, burlesque or comic distortion of slave plantation performance culture, African-American minstrels were often perceived by colonial Australians as just playing their African-American selves—mildly exotic and inherently amusing live exhibits. For example, 'REAL COLORED MEN From the Slave States of America, [who] will Appear in an ENTERTAINMENT, Portraying the peculiarities of Negro Life on the Plantation' (*Newcastle Morning Herald and Miners' Advocate*, 1876, p. 5–6) or 'Their movements are very fantastic, and they bound from their seats and play their bones and tambourines in attitudes that none but india rubber [sic] men or marionnettes could imitate … and crack jokes with a gusto seldom witnessed among white men' (*South Australian Chronicle and Weekly Mail*, 1877, p. 15).

Various all-black minstrel companies, or so-called 'Georgia' companies, with white or African-American managers toured Australia between 1876 and 1914 (see Figure 3.3) and African-American 'jubilee ('Negro spiritual' singing) companies also toured over the same period (and later) with considerable appeal to colonial Christians. The Georgia companies also featured 'Negro spirituals' but often hammed up to amuse their colonial audiences (Abbott and Seroff, 2007, pp. 21–22). The Georgia companies

---

[5] Even then, colonial critics often complained that troupe members were 'piebald' and not uniformly pitch-black like blackface minstrels.

were also hired for numerous local productions of the immensely popular melodrama, 'Uncle Tom's Cabin', in which they played black roles and presented slave plantation music and dance scenes with jubilee singing, slave field songs, banjo playing and improvisatory so-called 'plantation walk-around' dancing (Waterhouse, 1991, pp. 70–74). By the time the first Georgia minstrels reached Australia, local and touring white minstrel companies were de-emphasising the more jazz-like 'old-time slave plantation' music and dance aspects of their shows. However, this was kept alive as a plantation-life specialty of the black Georgia companies.

- 1876–1877: Sheradan Corbyn's Original Georgia Minstrels
- 1877–1880: Charles B. Hicks Georgia Minstrels
- 1881–1883: Mastodon Colored Minstrels: 60 artists including most of the Original Georgia Minstrels
- 1886–1889: Loudin's Fisk Jubilee Singers
- 1888–1891: Hicks-Sawyer Minstrels
- 1890–1920s: Orpheus McAdoo's Virginia Concert Party and Jubilee Singers (with personnel and name changes)
- June 1899–1900: McAdoo's Georgia Minstrels and Alabama Cakewalkers and Brass Band; Curtis' Afro-American Minstrel Carnival and Brass Band
- December 1912 – December 1913: Hugo's Colored Minstrels
- 1914: Hugo's New Minstrels (included white Australians).

Figure 3.3: Black minstrel and jubilee companies in Australia, 1876–1914
Source: Abbott and Seroff (2007) and Waterhouse (1991).

At the end of the 1880s, the Hicks-Sawyer company introduced the new so-called 'coon-song' and urban-themed 'hot coon' stereotype to Australia. Coon-song became immensely popular but also increasingly depicted urban African-Americans as flashy, gluttonous, gambling-addicted, ugly, 'uppity', razor-wielding, oversexed and excitingly rhythmic (Whitcomb, 1987, p. 100). In 1899, McAdoo's Georgia Minstrels and Alabama Cakewalkers and Curtis' Afro-American Minstrel Carnival introduced the new 'ragtime' and cakewalk-style minstrelsy to Australia (Whiteoak, 1999, pp. 116–134). Coon-song had become a vehicle for ragtime syncopation and improvisatory vocal ragging and its verse/chorus structure invited 'hot' ragged chorus accompaniment.

While the music and dance of the Georgias was often essentialised by Australian observers as naturally spontaneous, improvisatory and comedic, this perception is even more apparent in the numerous Australasian reviews of touring jubilee singing and jubilee/variety troupes collated in Abbott and Seroff (2002). The authors point out that because Australasian audiences were unfamiliar with the 'peculiarities and conventions of

African-American culture', they interpreted improvisatory musical gestures and expressive physical movement as 'comedic' or 'ludicrous, ridiculous, and humorous' (Abbott and Seroff, 2002, pp. 21–22).

Black minstrelsy enriched Australian popular entertainment with the presence and influence of many world-famous stars of African-American minstrel music, dance, comedy and variety. They included Japanese Tommy (Thomas Dilverd), minstrel and minstrelsy entrepreneur Charles Hicks, Billy Wilson, Sam Keenan, Billy Crusoe, Billy Speed, banjo virtuoso Hosea Easton, Charlie Pope, Irving Sales, cakewalkers Charles W. Walker and Ida May, Billy McClain, vocal ragtime and ragging pioneer Ernest Hogan, Billy Brown, Billy Kersands and Eva Taylor of later blues and jazz singing fame. Easton, Pope, Sales, Keenan, Brown and various others remained in Australia after their troupes had broken up or returned to North America; they became very popular in Australian minstrelsy-related entertainment (Waterhouse, 1991, pp. 93–95).

Minstrel Bands and Orchestras

The most tantalising feature of the black minstrel companies from a later 'jazz in Australia' perspective is their strikingly costumed black minstrel parade and concert brass bands, which also played for the minstrel show, especially as these were exactly the same type of pre-jazz black ensembles that are exhaustively documented in Abbott and Seroff's (2007) *Ragged but Right: Black Traveling Shows, 'Coon Songs,' and the Dark Pathways to Blues and Jazz*.

Corbyn's Georgia Minstrels (1876–77) only carried a drum and fife parade band (*Launceston Examiner*, 1877, p. 3), but the Hicks, Mastodon, Hicks-Sawyer and later black companies carried popular 'brass' (brass and woodwind) parade/concert bands that (with doubling on strings) became minstrel-show orchestras accompanied by the noisy rattling of bones and tambourines. Colonial reviews and advertisements often provide detailed information about the size and instrumentation of the bands, their colourful parade uniforms, who led them, what items they played and even the names of many of the performers. These reviews rarely describe music performance practice or performance behaviour. Thus, circumstantial evidence must be relied on to determine what sorts of idiomatically African-American or other participatory discrepancies, or incipient ragging and jazzing, the musicians might have brought to their music to fulfil the white public's expectations of the 'ludicrous' comic musical distortion of the 'happy' and rhythmic musical 'darkie' at play. Did the black bands that reached Australia, for example, feature a mix of untrained ear-playing and trained reading musicians as in legends about the origins of New Orleans jazz?

Such questions become even more important when considering the late 1890s, when the syncopated ragtime subgenres, cakewalk-march music and coon-song entered minstrel band repertoires. A further problem is uncertainty, in the absence of confirming evidence on record, about the precise nature of the music of New Orleans (or other US locations) that became, retrospectively, known as 'jazz' in the 1910s, or about how this early 'jazz' or 'jazzing' might have differed from black bands playing and enthusiastically embellishing or 'ragging' the new syncopated ragtime subgenres.

An important early example of wind band ragging is the attention-grabbing circus trombone 'smears', 'glisses' or 'rags' (later called 'jazzes') of cakewalk-march music. Trombone historian Rick Benjamin states that 'dating back to the 1870s … white performers in blackface used the trombone as a raucous noisemaker to somehow assist in their "evocations" of plantation life' (cited in Wondrich, 2003, pp. 75–76). Cakewalk-marches are composed and arranged music, but in *Stomp and Swerve: American Music Gets Hot, 1843–1924*, David Wondrich (2003) demonstrates through musicological analysis of examples, such as Arthur Pryor's 1902 recording of 'Trombone Sneeze: A Humoresque Cakewalk' played by the famous Sousa band,[6] that even a conservative white wind band could bring surprisingly jazz-like freedom to its performances of this genre (pp. 63–81).

Being parade bands that functioned to attract public attention and patronage from far away to the minstrel show, there is no doubt that minstrel musicians, like circus musicians, could play very loudly. Even when functioning as minstrel orchestras, they were sometimes censured for being sonically overpowering (*The Queenslander*, 1888, p. 752). There is also an intriguing reference to the Hicks-Sawyer band in a tune-for-tune volume 'battle' with the famous Australian Wirth's Circus band (Wirth, 1925, p. 45); the ability to play exceptionally loud is central to the murky myth of the early New Orleans trumpeter Buddy Bolden considered by many as the 'Father of Jazz' (Marquis, 2005, p. 70).

---

6   Hear this at youtube.com/watch?v=P3NU7LGBDcA (accessed 23 March 2016).

Published Australian observations of the black minstrel band musicians often give the impression that they were well trained and disciplined in music and marching in an era when the modern brass or mixed brass and reeds band was central to Australian public popular entertainment and organised amateur music making (Whiteoak, 2001, pp. 27–48). Therefore, these critics were in a suitable position to compare the quality of the black minstrel bands with the leading Australian amateur, volunteer, circus and other commercial bands of the era:

> There are many in Hobart who can remember the Hicks-Sawyer Minstrel Band, which paraded from the Theatre Royal daily decked in darktown rig, and at the head of which was a drum major who skied his staff away up into the heavens, and caught it the same way in various gymnastic shapes. History once stated that thick-lipped musicians were no good on brass instruments, especially the cornet. Well, that theory was killed when these coloured stars got on the job. But eight or nine of them, they fairly shook the town, and their music, well it made lads and lassies leave the counter and workshop it was of such an enticing and gripping character. To say darkies have no soul. The Hick-Sawyer troupe proved [this to be a lie]. (*Critic*, 1917, p. 6)

Where the names of minstrel company band members are known, it can be shown that many also doubled as star comedians, vocalists, buck and wing dancers, or variety act artists (see Figure 3.4).

- Henderson Smith Leader, solo Bb cornet (*and M.D. for the show*)
- Jessie E. Smith, solo Bb cornet
- James P. Jones, solo clarinet
- James Harris, first trombone
- Alonzo Edwards, second trombone
- Oscar Lindsay, solo alto horn
- John Brewer, first alto horn (*and sketches, cakewalker, buck and wing dancing*)
- Pete Woods, baritone horn (*other role unknown*)
- Edward Tolliver, tuba (*and juggler*)
- Turner Jones, bass drum (*and juggler*)
- Frank Poole, snare drum (*and sketches*)
- Jackson Heard, cymbals (*and sketches*)
- George Henry, drum major (*other role unknown*)
- John Pamplin, lightning gun driller (*and juggler*).

Figure 3.4: The McAdoo Company Brass Band and Orchestra, 1899

Source: Derived from listing of McAdoo Company personnel and their roles in Abbott and Seroff (2002, Appendix 2, p. 464).

This mirrored the situation of the travelling Australian family circus bands of that period, which necessarily brought skilled professional musicians together with untrained musicians/circus performers (who could not necessarily read music) in contexts requiring improvisatory musical interaction, such as in backing unpredictable variety acts (Whiteoak, 1999, pp. 69–82). Irving Sales, a leading minstrel comedian and coon-song and minstrel dance artist in the 1880s Hicks-Sawyer company, and later star comedian and 'coon-specialist' in Australian vaudeville, was especially recalled by a journalist as having been the slide trombonist in the Hicks-Sawyer street parades (Day, 1917, p. 14). What, if any, flamboyant, attention-grabbing liberties or 'razzamatazz' this gifted black minstrel/comedian/slide trombonist brought to his street-parade playing must remain a matter of speculation.

All brass bands carried by the black minstrel companies featured one or several star instrumentalists to boost the repute of the band and appear as soloists. The 14-member brass band of the 1899–1900 McAdoo Georgia Minstrel and Cakewalkers was led by a very famous conductor and cornet soloist, Professor Henderson Smith, known in America as 'the black Sousa' (Abbott and Seroff, 2002, p. 128). Rival Curtis' Afro-American Minstrel Carnival company featured the 'Famous Kansas City Pickaninny Band', an acclaimed 16-member teenage band led by Professor Nathaniel Clark Smith (*Brisbane Courier*, 1900, 2),[7] who is credited with training jazz musicians such as Walter Page, Harlen Leonard, Leroy Maxey and the legendary Wilbur C. Sweatman, who Berresford believes was a member of the Pickaninny Band during its Australasian tour (Berresford, 2010, pp. 21–24).[8] A program published in Kansas City soon after the Australasian tour bills the Pickaninny Band as presenting 'A Ragtime Concert given in front of the [Grand Opera House] each evening'(Londré, 2007, p. 207), remembering that use of the term 'jazz' in popular music was still more than a decade away.

Both minstrel bands had departed Australasia by May 1901 and, disappointingly, numerous reviews of both companies fail to detail what ragging, participatory discrepancies or other razzamatazz they brought to their music as parade or concert bands playing cakewalk-marches, coon-songs and other early ragtime or cakewalk-era popular music. Similarly,

---

7   See also Abbott and Seroff (2002, pp. 403–409).
8   See a Pickaninny Band image at images.fineartamerica.com/images/artworkimages/mediumlarge/1/old-kentucky-the-original-pickaninny-band-1894-r-muirhead-art.jpg (accessed 25 March 2016).

they reveal very little about how, as orchestras, they accompanied black dancing, coon-song and 'rag-time opera' in the dynamic comic-distortion 'mirth factory' context of ragtime minstrelsy.

Some Circumstantial Evidence

The most common terms used to describe the parade bands' music were 'enlivening', 'spirited' or 'stirring'. For example:

> Twenty [black minstrels] turned out with their champion brass band, marching through all the leading streets, and performing various spirit-stirring airs in masterly style ... followed by admiring crowds, and all doors, windows, and sidewalks were crowded with astonished spectators. (*The Cornwall Chronicle*, 1877, p. 2)

By the late 1890s, however, ragging or ragtime improvising (including the trombone 'smears' or 'rags' associated with cakewalk-march music) was already becoming codified in 'how to rag' instructors and notated representations of ragging in Tin Pan Alley scores (Harney, 1897; Whiteoak, 1999, pp. 111–67). In fact, world-famous coon-song ragger, comedian and composer Ernest Hogan, who headed the Curtis company, had produced a massive global coon-song hit in 1896, published with both straight and optional ragged chorus accompaniment.[9] Novelty or unorthodox noise-making and musical burlesque or clowning had always been part of the comedic appeal of minstrelsy and, in the case of black minstrels, being comedic was perceived by many to be a natural and expected attribute. Minstrelsy had always been a context for improvisatory music practices. Furthermore, among the minstrel musicians were concert soloists with an excess of musical ability, such as clarinettist James P. Jones or solo cornet players Frank Hewett, Charles Bruce, Jessie P. Smith and Henderson Smith, who probably performed cadenzas or variations on the parade band tunes, which they knew by heart.[10] The Kansas Pickaninny Band leader Nathaniel Clark Smith is a legendary figure in jazz education history; it is likely that famous jazz pioneer Sweatman was in Australia as a band member (Berresford, 2010, p. 24).

---

9   'All Coons Look Alike to Me: a Darkey Misunderstanding'. 1896. New York: M. Witmark & Sons.
10 Also argued in Lewis (2012, p. 41).

Despite the very modest commercial success of these two large black minstrel companies, there is no doubt of their significance in exposing Australian audiences to the new syncopated and improvisatory ragtime music and dance genres and the way they were performed by black artists.[11] Circumstantial evidence points to the probability that the band and orchestra music was playfully embellished in ways that would be recognised, today, as incipient jazzing.

'T'ain't What You Do (It's the Way That You Do It)'[12]

'Real' Ragtime

The last large-scale black minstrel company to tour Australia, Hugo's Colored Minstrels, arrived in late 1912 led by world-famous minstrel Billy Kersands, and featuring genuine 'old-time minstrelsy' ragtime dancers, a 'Real Ragtime Band' (*Daily Herald*, 1912a, p. 2) and Leah Clarke, an Amazonian lady 'rag-shouter' who sang 'to beat the band' and got audiences 'jiggin' with her hot interpretations of the latest ragtime hits (*The Mail*, 1912, p. 3; *The Register*, 1912, p. 5). During the long but ultimately ill-fated tour, company members were refused accommodation on colour 'taboo' grounds, bashed by racist thugs and ostracised by the gutter press for entertaining white women in a scandal that preceded the infamous 'Colored Idea' scandal by 17 years (*Albury Banner and Wodonga Express*, 1912, p. 20; *Truth*, 1912, p. 5).

Clarke's 'singing to beat the band' anticipated the novelty of the two equally Amazonian white 'rag-shouters' who respectively led and competed, volume-wise, with 'Australia's First Jazz Band' six years later (Whiteoak, 1994, p. 289). Descriptions of the Hugo company's breezy music and dance extravaganza finale, called 'Alexander's Ragtime Band' resemble another extravaganza called 'Alexander's Jazz Band', presented in a Sydney revue months before the 1918 Jazz Band. However, the 'Real Ragtime Band' feature is of particular interest from a jazz perspective.

---

11 However, the degree to which the minstrel musicians were actually, to quote Abbott and Serroff (2002, p. 451), 'asserting an African-American cultural sensibility' in their playing is a far more difficult problem.
12 Common saying in show business and title of a 1939 jazz song by Melvin Oliver and James Young.

An important clue to the existence of a new, unfamiliar and special quality about this 'real' ragtime band is its highly publicised claim that it would demonstrate to Australians 'how Irving Berlin's "Everybody's Doing It" and "Alexander's Ragtime Band" should be played', or in other words, ragged or otherwise transformed by African Americans into 'real ragtime' (*Daily Herald*, 1912b, p. 3).

Therefore, we have to momentarily return to Lacan and the word 'real' itself as a placeholder, since there is no certainty about what 'real ragtime band' signified in an early 1910s context in which the term 'real jazz band' would not have conveyed anything to Australian patrons. Yet it is easy to imagine—and even accept— that this real ragtime music, played showily in the street parade or in the final chorus of Clarke's ragging as she competed with the band to get her audience jiggin', brought something excitingly different to Australian musical entertainment. This was probably something that was not heard again live until the end of Australia's Jazz Age, with the short and ill-fated visit of the black jazz band of the Colored Idea Company called, ironically, a Plantation Orchestra (Johnson, 2010).

The Hugo's Colored Minstrels tour essentially ended a three-and-a-half-decade era in which African-American artists contributed directly to the shaping and content of popular music in Australia through their art and through what many white Australians artists learnt from them as collaborators, observers or students (Waterhouse, 1991, pp. 93–95). If we put aside the demeaning comic racial mocking inherent in minstrelsy as mainstream popular entertainment, it becomes possible to argue that Australia was, in fact, part of a 'good black music story'. However, after the *Immigration Restriction Act 1901* was enacted to exclude 'coloured races' from gaining residency, an increasingly xenophobic Australian society discarded the opportunity to remain part of a story that could have enriched our popular music culture and our jazz scene in priceless ways. Even by the 1950s, the Musicians Union remained divided about removing Clause 1 of its constitutional objectives to 'uphold the White Australia policy, and prohibit the admission of coloured races' in deference to the musical contribution of black jazz greats (Webberley, 1952, p. 21).

Abbott and Seroff (2002, p. 137) note:

> More than one hundred black American entertainers witnessed the dawn of the twentieth century under Australasian skies, and among them were the cream of the vaudeville and minstrel stage. There were nearly as many first-rate black acts in Australia at this time as there were back in the States.

The constellation of major and minor black stars that orbited across the vista of Australian entertainment between the 1870s and World War One has already been recognised as a 'good black story' within Australian theatre studies.[13] However, it has largely failed to catch the attention or interest of Australian jazz scholarship or, more surprisingly, the broader field of popular music studies. It is hoped that this initial musical investigation will encourage music scholarship that can penetrate the foggy gloom of white embarrassment about racial mocking and reveal a good black music story deserving of a rightful and dignified place in our popular music history.

References

Abbott, L. and D. Seroff. 2002. *Out of Sight: The Rise of African American Popular Music, 1889–1895*. Jackson: University Press of Mississippi.

——. 2007. *Ragged but Right: Black Traveling Shows, 'Coon Songs,' and the Dark Pathway to Blues and Jazz*. Jackson: University Press of Mississippi.

Albury Banner and Wodonga Express. 1912. 'Blacks Tabood'. 6 December, 20.

Bailly, L. 2009. *Lacan: A Beginner's Guide*. Oxford: Oneworld.

Berlin, E. A. 1980. *Ragtime: A Musical and Cultural History*. Berkeley: University of California Press.

Berresford, M. 2010. *That's Got Em: The Life and Music of Wilbur Sweatman*. Jackson: University Press of Mississippi. doi.org/10.14325/mississippi/9781604730999.001.0001

---

13 For example, see entries on black minstrels in Australian Variety Theatre Archive at ozvta.com/ or Waterhouse (1991, pp. 61–97).

Brisbane Courier. 1900. 'Entertainments'. 11 January, 2.

Brooks, T. 2004. *Lost Sounds: Blacks and the Birth of the Recording Industry, 1890–1919*. Urbana and Chicago: University of Illinois Press.

Burns, K. (Director) 2001. *Jazz: A Film by Ken Burns*. Florentine Films and WETA.

Critic. 1917. 'Trombone: Bands and Bandsmen'. 9 March, 6.

Daily Herald. 1912a. 'At the Theatre Royal'. 30 November, 2.

———. 1912b. 'Hugo's Minstrels'. 30 November, 3.

Day, V. 1917. 'The Stage'. *Referee*. 25 July, 14.

Gennari, J. 2006. *Blowin' Hot and Cool: Jazz and Its Critics*. Chicago: University of Chicago Press. doi.org/10.7208/chicago/9780226289243.001.0001

Gushee, L. 2005. *Pioneers of Jazz: The Story of the Creole Band*. New York: Oxford University Press.

Handy, W. C. 1970. *Father of the Blues: An Autobiography*. Edited by Arna Bontemps. New York: Collier Books.

Harney, B. 1897. *Ben Harney's Rag Time Instructor*. Chicago: Sol Bloom.

Johnson, B. 2010. 'Deportation Blues: Black Jazz and White Australia in the 1920s'. *Journal for the International Society for the Study of Popular Music* 1 (1): 1–13. doi.org/10.5429/2079-3871(2010)v1i1.5en

Keil, C. 1994. 'Participatory Discrepancies and the Power of Music'. In *Music Grooves: Essays and Dialogues*, edited by C. Keil and S. Feld, 96–108. Chicago: University of Chicago Press.

Launceston Examiner. 1877. 'Georgia Minstrels'. 11 September, 3.

Lewis, S. 2012. '"Untamed Music": Early Jazz in Vaudeville'. Honours thesis, Florida State University. diginole.lib.fsu.edu/islandora/object/fsu%3A204554 (accessed 23 March 2016).

Londré, F. H. 2007. *The Enchanted Years of the Stage: Kansas City at the Crossroads of American Theatre 1870–1930*. Columbia: University of Missouri Press.

Lotz, E. 1997. *Black People: Entertainers of African Descent in Europe and Germany*. Bonn, Germany: Birgit Lotz-Verlag.

Marquis, D. M. 2005. *In Search of Buddy Bolden: First Man of Jazz*. Rev. ed. Baton Rouge: Louisiana State University Press.

Newcastle Morning Herald and Miners' Advocate. 1876. 'Amusements'. 16 December, 5–6.

Pond, S. 2003. 'Jamming the Reception: Ken Burns, "Jazz", and the Problem of "America's Music"'. *Quarterly Journal of the Music Library Association* 60 (1): 11–45. doi.org/10.1353/not.2003.0124

Radano, R. 2003. *Lying up a Nation: Race and Black Music*. Chicago: University of Chicago Press.

Reiner, T. 2015. 'Approaching Music Through Language: A Lacanian Perspective'. Paper presented at the Symposium on Perspectives on Artistic Research in Music, Monash University, July.

South Australian Chronicle and Weekly Mail. 1877. 'The Georgia Minstrels'. 13 October, 15.

The Advertiser. 1918. 'The Majestic Theatre'. 19 August, 7.

The Cornwall Chronicle. 1877. 'The Georgia Minstrels'. 8 August, 2.

The Mail. 1912. 'Hugo's Minstrels'. 14 December, 3.

The Queenslander. 1888. 'Her Majesty's Opera House Hicks-Sawyer Minstrels'. 27 October, 752.

The Register. 1912. 'Amusements'. 16 December, 5.

Truth. 1912. 'Black Bucks and White Wantons'. 23 November, 5.

Waterhouse, R. 1991. *From Minstrel Show to Vaudeville: the Australian Popular Stage 1788–1914*. Kensington, NSW: New South Wales University Press.

Webberley, M. 1952. 'Notice of Motion to Hobart Branch of Musicians' Union of Australia'. *Music Maker*. August, 20.

Whitcomb, I. 1987. *Irving Berlin and Ragtime America*. London: Century Hutchinson.

Whiteoak, J. 1994. '"Jazzing" and Australia's First Jazz Band'. *Popular Music* 13 (3): 279–295. doi.org/10.1017/S0261143000007200

———. 1999. *Playing Ad Lib: Improvisatory Music in Australia, 1836–1970*. Sydney: Currency Press.

———. 2001. 'Popular Music, Militarism, Women and the Early "Brass Band" in Australia'. *Australasian Music Research* 6: 27–48.

———. 2014. 'Demons of Discord Down Under: From "Jump Jim Crow" to "Australia's First Jazz Band"'. *Jazz Research Journal* 8 (1–2): 23–51.

Wirth, G. 1925. *Round the World with a Circus: Memories of Trials and Tribulations*. Melbourne: Troedel & Cooper.

Wondrich, D. 2003. *Stomp and Swerve: American Music Gets Hot, 1843–1924*. Chicago: Chicago Review Press.

4

'You're Messin' Up My Mind': Why Judy Jacques Avoided the Path of the Pop Diva

Robin Ryan

Introduction: Stardom and Talent

This chapter puts forward a conceptual framework for a 'stardom in flux' illustrated through the internal and external growth of a single female career. With a freakish vocal range spanning C below middle-C to high E-flat, the singer-songwriter Judy Jacques (born in Melbourne, 1944) has progressively manifested varying forms of stardom moderated by the biases of popular culture. In view of the niche scenes and musical movements outlined below, I propose that a stardom in flux may represent society in flux as much as a life in flux. In contrast to a hypothetical 'steady-state stardom', the complex social relations, stylistic trajectories and geographical contexts that hinge around a stardom in flux prove to be many and varied.

Talent, defined by McLeod and Herndon (1980, p. 188), is 'the concept of an innate predisposition to competence'. It was a compulsion for singing that propelled the young Jacques into the limelight of Melbourne's jazz/folk boom and gospel circuits. Riding on her success in 1960s television, she was on the cusp of becoming the pin-up 'Olivia' or 'Kylie' of her day—had it not been for a crisis point when the singer baulked at the barriers being put up around female artists. Jacques diverged to an experimental phase that established her as 'one of the most technically competent vocalists in Australia' (Johnson, 1987, p. 58) and, more specifically, as 'one of Australia's most adventurous improvising jazz vocalists' (Whiteoak, 2008, p. 44).

I began to research the subject in 2001 and collected context-specific performance data in Melbourne and Flinders Island, Bass Strait. Informed by the binary opposition between commerce and creativity moderated by Negus (1995), the case study highlights the anxieties germane to the commodification of female musical identity practices in the 1960s at local, state, national and transitory international levels revolving around the tensions of 'local' versus 'big star' culture. As Negus (1995) points out, a celebrity dynamic may include interplay between commerce and creativity as well as discontinuity.

Jacques' critiques of the systems within which she worked in stage, screen and studio furnish previously unpublished information in a periodisation for how she achieved an unusually fluid experience of singing, and of how—in an ironic twist—her 1966 Northern Soul pop single 'You're Messin' Up My Mind' found its way back onto high rotation. New slants on the character of Jacques' times and contemporary cultural forms other than pop emerge in the following overview (see Ryan [2014] for a more detailed biographical account).

Teenage Jazz Stardom

In 1952, eight-year-old Judy Jacques delivered a performance of 'Smoke Gets in Your Eyes' at a Pakenham hotel. By age 11, she was a regular performer on Radio 3AW. Determined to be a professional singer, Jacques left school at 14 to perform country songs and pop hits by Bill Haley, the Everly Brothers and Elvis Presley with her sister Yvonne (The Two Jays). In 1958, the fledgling Yarra Yarra New Orleans Jazz Band (henceforth The Yarras) were offered the Saturday night dance at Moorabbin Scout Hall on the condition that 15-year-old Jacques could retain her regular appearances.

Initially, a couple of the men—who did not want a 'sheila' in the band—attempted to discourage Jacques by calling her a 'good pop singer'. Displaying a precocious degree of female agency, Jacques returned each night until she was accepted as central to the band's 'sound'. Her local self-made stardom became a form of consumption negotiated by fan communities. As Eric Brown (n.d.) writes, 'In later years she was to become so popular that she even became a cult figure. In 1963 every girl in Melbourne seemed to be wearing her hair in Judy's style—long with a fringe in front'. In a mediation of female body perception, television reviewers described Jacques as 'refreshing' since her healthy-looking, shiny hairstyle (see Figure 4.1) prevailed in an era when female performers backcombed their hair into lacquered 'beehives'.[1]

Figure 4.1: Fans surround Judy Jacques at Jazz as You Like It, Melbourne Town Hall, 1963
Source: Photo by Bruce Anderson, courtesy Judy Jacques Collection.

Jacques nevertheless determined to establish her voice as the trademark of her rising stardom:

> I had the idea that if I held on to being true to myself then I would develop the same in my music. I was also aware that the huge majority of musicians were men, and most treated girl singers as decoration. I was

---

1   Jacques claims that her 'look' preceded that of Mary Travers, to whom she was to be compared in the heyday of the Great Australian Cringe (email to the author, 11 October 2016).

determined to prove my worth as a musician, as I gradually understood that female singers got gigs because they looked good or sexy in front of a band. Even back then, that made me very angry and I didn't 'glam up' until I was quite a mature singer. (email to the author, 26 November 2015)

Bandleader Maurice Garbutt[2] nurtured the young Jacques in the art of improvisation by testing her ability to change key mid-song, to cope with extended blues progressions and invent her own lyrics on stage—tactics that taught her to think about the 'inside' of the music. A leading player in Melbourne's early 1960s trad-jazz boom, The Yarras performed at Australian Jazz Conventions in Melbourne (1960), Adelaide (1961) and Sydney (1962).[3] In 1962, they shared Downbeat and Jazz at City Hall concerts with a newly formed folk vocal group, which—in a meteoric rise to fame—were to become the first Australian group to clinch a UK number one (Bartlett, 2015, p. 15). At one of these performances, The Seekers invited Jacques to join them in advance of their overseas venture but she graciously declined because she was committed to learning more about Black American blues, gospel and jazz from The Yarras' purism:

> Those were early days, and I felt I was on a journey of sorts, knowing I had a long way to go. Joining The Seekers would have been a very sharp right-hand turn. I've never regretted that decision. (email to the author, 4 December 2015)

Marcus Herman, who operated the local independent Crest label for just over a decade, recorded a broad range of material from jazz to blues, pop and organ music (Australian Broadcasting Corporation [ABC], 2013a). Herman produced The Yarras' first recording in 1962, followed by a live LP recording of the Moomba Lunch Hour Concert Jazz as You Like it (see Figure 4.1) in 1963. At the same time, Jacques' youthful celebrity status was taking an independent side turn.

---

2   Garbutt led the band's original line-up of Bob Brown, Eddie Robbins and Lee Treanor.
3   The Yarras staged a crowded weekly dance at Gas Works in Kew Town Hall, played at Jazz Centre 44 in St Kilda and ran the Yarra Yarra N.O. Jazz Centre punt in South Yarra. Traditional jazz flourished as an alternative to rock, with Melbourne teenagers confrontationally divided along the lines of 'jazzers' versus 'rockers'—that is, until surf music and the Beatles came to dominate popular music (see Gaudion, in Sharpe, 2008, pp. 125–156).

Gospel Pioneering Stardom

Jacques was introducing songs from the black gospel canon to mainstream Australia by age 18, well before the genre infiltrated the repertoires of church groups and choirs nationwide. To set the pace, Judy Jacques and her Gospel Four (Australia's first popular gospel group) toured Victoria and released a 45 EP with Crest in 1963. Conventional ministers of religion complained to the press about her style of singing. However, with the benefit of hindsight, *RareCollections* presenters Jordie and David Kilby have described Jacques as being 'without doubt one of the finest gospel singers to ever cut a record in Australia, the proof being in her great reading of the standard "Didn't It Rain Children"' (ABC, 2013a). In 1964, Segue recorded a new line-up of Jacques' group performing four tracks on the 45 EP, *Be My Friend*.[4] A GTV 9 producer featured Jacques on *In Melbourne Tonight* (*IMT*), and she went on to freelance with all television channels.

Jazz and folk clubs flourished 'cheek by jowl' in 1960s Melbourne. The idioms connected for Jacques in offering an alternative to the blander popular songs of the 1950s and 1960s. Warming to the activist sense of responsibility in folk music, she stayed behind to mix with folk singers whenever The Yarras performed in coffee bars. Besides extending her repertoire, Jacques formed a productive relationship with the fine interpretive singer Margret RoadKnight. At barely 19 years, Jacques used her economic success to purchase a farm north-east of Melbourne at St Andrews, where she entertained the acclaimed American trio Peter, Paul and Mary (formed in 1961 during the folk music revival phenomenon) during their 1964 Australian tour:

> We sang and ate and Mary Travers rode my horse, Big Boy Pete. They talked about this amazing young singer-songwriter Bob Dylan, and I suspect their concerts introduced him to Australia. I attended their Festival Hall concert as their guest. They were very impressive on stage, tight and shiny, but with integrity as well. They made folk accessible and popular. (Jacques, cited in Ryan, 2014, p. 7)

Later in the year, the original cast of *Black Nativity* (renamed in Australia *Go Tell it on the Mountain*) arrived at 'Wild Dog Hill' for a barbeque: Alex Bradford, Princess Stewart and the entire Patterson Singers.

---

4   Jacques remained attached to gospel, performing in The Angels of Soul, Calling All Angels and Judy Jacques' Sweet Rosetta Band in the mid to late 2000s.

In Jacques' words:

> They just gathered around my piano and away we went! Their magnificent voices are still with me … I just couldn't believe that they were in my house, far less me singing with them! Alex invited Margret and I to his 30th birthday party at Southern Cross Hotel: another night of unforgettable gospel music. (cited in Ryan, 2014, p. 7)

In the wake of these breathtaking experiences, Jacques began to feel uncomfortable with the way that television was squeezing her into a pop-diva mould.

Commodity Pop Stardom

Commenting on the *thinness* of the experiences that commercial art offers to women, Frith (1996, p. 19, 213) observed how '[t]he female performer is inevitably much more self-conscious than a male performer in that she has to keep redefining both her performing space and her performing narrative if she is to take charge of her situation'. The structures of contemporary pop culture invited a reaction (and eventual revolt) on the part of the young Jacques as she flirted for a short period with teenage television shows. She chose vocally challenging items of 'soul' in preference to 'pop': 'Burt Bacharach, Aretha Franklin, Dionne Warwick to name a few … not just to be different, but because I thought they were musically more interesting' (Jacques, email to the author, 11 October 2016).

Mid-1960s celebrity branding was the exclusive domain of the industry. When Channel 9 producers asked Jacques to sing more 'accessible' songs, she was faced with the choice of either dropping out of television or coming up with something better than donning a hairpiece to sing 'rocked-up' quasi-gospel songs to the sound of backing singers, far removed from the rousing gospel music that she loved. So, in 1966, when ABC2 invited the singer to add a fresh image to their *Dig We Must* television series, it was perfect timing: 'the beginning of checking out a bigger, more versatile world' (Jacques, email to the author, 26 November 2015).

Jacques co-compered two series with Idris Jones for ABC TV's *Start Living*. She also performed gospel items on *Bandstand*, including *Live at the Myer Music Bowl* in 1965. In the 'bigger, more versatile world' of the late 1960s, she supported Johnny O'Keefe concerts at Pentridge Prison and in Sydney clubs: 'I liked John, loathed the clubs, and wouldn't do anymore!' (Jacques, email to the author, 11 October 2016).[5] The singer also shared an ABC radio series with Ronnie Burns and cut a recording with The Idlers Five. To accommodate a pop image and attitude, Jacques designed braided linen pants with a silk ruffle-fronted shirt to be worn under an open jacket—something a little 'artier' than the 'glam' gowns worn by her contemporaries. In an example of how stardom buys leverage, designers and boutique owners supplied Jacques with clothes in exchange for acknowledgements in her show credits, and sometimes allowed her to keep the garments (email to the author, 26 November 2015). Ron Tudor from Astor Records invited Jacques to record two pop singles for the commercial market in 1966. She selected 'You're Messin' Up My Mind', cut by Herb Fame and produced by its composer Van McCoy for Blackwood, BMI. Peter Robinson and John Farrar from The Strangers produced the 45 rpm single with 'Since You're Gone', written by Bobby Darin, on the B-side.[6] Jacques recorded the song at Bill Armstrong Studios on the Astor label (see Figures 4.2 and 4.3) and, in the words of ABC Radio National (2013b), 'made it her own'.

Figures 4.2 and 4.3: Jacques Records 'You're Messin' Up My Mind' at Armstrong Studios, 1966
Source: Images by Mary Thompson, courtesy Judy Jacques Collection.

---

5   While working with O'Keefe, Jacques sang hits like 'Leaving on a Jet Plane' on *Bandstand*.
6   Playback Records producer Nathan Impiombato (email to the author, 19 November 2015) supports the view of Jacques and the National Film and Sound Archive, Canberra, that the single was recorded in 1966 rather than 1967 (cited by the Australian Broadcasting Commission, 2013b).

Jacques played the record 'full bore' at parties; however, her producer thought it a risky choice, and correctly predicted that it would not achieve good airplay in Australia because it sounded 'too Black' (Jacques, email to the author, 13 April 2015). In 1969, Jacques submitted a tape of original David Langdon songs to Ron Tudor, who returned it on 20 December 1969 with a letter, commenting:

> For some reason or other this record business seems to have a jinx for girl singers ... David has a real Bacharach 'feel' to some of his songs, and while this is admirable in many respects it can also be dangerous because many songs of this calibre just miss out on mass acceptance in this country. (Letter from Heathmont, Victoria)

Northern Soul Stardom

Paradoxically, the driving rhythm and horn arrangement in 'You're Messin' Up My Mind' made it perfect for British dance floors (ABC, 2013b). Thus, Jacques' name took root within the vital Northern Soul scene that emerged in the Manchester in the late 1960s. Journalist Dave Godin coined the label following a visit to the Twisted Wheel nightclub to describe a distinctive brand of music that could not be found in London clubs at the time (charly.co.uk, n.d.).[7] Jacques personally describes Northern Soul as 'a play on the label "Southern Soul"—the blues from down south USA and all its influences' (email to the author, 17 November 2015).

The Northern Soul scene exhibited the typical traits of a cult movement as 'vibers' adopted their own dance moves, flamboyant clothing and haircuts. According to the ABC (2013b):

> As the all-nighter club crowds proliferated, so did the public appetite for new and increasingly obscure recordings. DJs looked abroad for fresh sounds, and over the years Australian singles by Lynne Randell, Cheryl Gray, Doug Parkinson and Judy Jacques developed a reputation amongst DJs and dancers alike.

These so-called 'obscure' cultural products were, of course, well established back in Australia.

---

7   Emanating from a Brazennose Street coffee bar, the Twisted Wheel relocated to a Whitworth Street warehouse in 1965. Its reputation for imported soul, R&B and ska saw fans flocking to hear live sets by artists of the ilk of Little Richard, Bo Diddley and Fats Domino. The famous Manchester club was bulldozed in January 2013 (Pidd, 2012).

Stardom or Free Singing?

Meanwhile, the notion of posing to gratify Australian audiences began, in a metaphorical sense, to 'mess' with Jacques' mind. Drained from constructing a façade of pop stardom, and in a type of leap into the void, the singer left television in late 1971 to assess her future artistic direction. Her desire to recapture the ecstatic feeling of being *at one* in the music propelled her into a delayed adolescence: 'What I was searching for needed to be let out and, somehow, it was let out in a wild and uncompromising way: an exhilarating period of personal and artistic growth' (Jacques, cited in Ryan, 2014, p. 8).

The late 1970s became a time of experimental thinking and doing for Jacques after saxophonist and big band leader Barry Veith and his colleagues at La Trobe University 'opened up her mind space' to the unrealised expressive potential of using her voice as an instrument. The singer's symbolic resistance to commodification characterised the thrust of the historic Clifton Hill Community Music Centre countermovement (1976–1983), in which participants engaged in challenging and confronting performances of collective free improvisation.

While this dissembling and reordering of Jacques' musical priorities could be understood as 'changing boxes for spheres' (after King, 1980, p. 170), it also suggests that a star persona is 'a performer for self' as well as 'a performer for others' (the audience). The singer developed a primal wordless language that found its expression in free-form opera, theatre, world-beat and a fermenting crucible of composition—albeit at the cost of career fragmentation.

Fallen Stardom, Restored Stardom

Frith (1996, p. 214) notes that performers always face the threat of the ultimate embarrassment: *the performance that doesn't work*. Jacques' atonal vocals mostly 'fell on deaf ears', alienating lovers of the 'standards' and even, on one occasion, inciting a riot. During an avant-garde performance at a late 1970s Christmas Hills music festival, a vociferous crowd ran towards the singer shouting obscenities and throwing cans. Metaphorically speaking, the star system had been struck as if by an asteroid. Historically speaking, the rise of 'new music' in Australia had sparked a cultural struggle. Jacques nevertheless persisted with the avant-garde into the

1990s. She recorded the LP *Winged Messenger* in 1987, inspiring Sigmund Jorgenson to commission Brian Brown's jazz/modal opera of the same title for the opening the 1994 Montsalvat Jazz Festival.

Inescapably, a stardom in flux was enacted between the singer's countercultural freedom and a pragmatic need, from 1972, to acquire a revenue stream from television. She spent time abroad with her family from 1974–75 and returned to Australia freshly inspired. In 1981, Jacques supported US trumpeter Dizzy Gillespie during his Melbourne tour; she performed with the Brian Brown Ensemble in Sydney in the late 1980s and—returning to an established jazz discourse—she joined the Yarra Yarra Reunion Band for part of their residency at Bell's Hotel, South Melbourne.

In the late 1990s, Jacques variously performed with High Steppin', Blues by Five, Blues on the Boil, and her own groups Judy Jacques Ensemble and Wild Dog Ensemble. Her formation of the band Judy Jacques' Lighthouse to compose and perform *Going for a Song* for the 1997 Edinburgh Festival Fringe was a more ambitious move, followed by a tour of Wales, Italy and France. Unable to survive free of commercial restraints, Jacques was successfully negotiating the aesthetic and the commercial (concept after Negus, 1995, p. 323), and—as the next phase confirms—reaching beyond experiences of a purely musical kind.

Mature Autonomous Stardom

Using her Bass Strait ancestral roots from 1835 as a referent for her identity, the singer redefined her artistic space to articulate the ecological, political and social history of Flinders Island (the largest island in Tasmania's Furneaux Group). In the domain-specific album *Making Wings* (2002), she blended original balladry, gospel and folk jazz with wordless improvisations, taped location sounds and revived Indigenous Tasmanian song. This free rein over her musical direction projected a more specialised star identity. The inaugural Australian Jazz Bell Awards (The Bells) delivered the Best Australian Jazz Vocal Album category to the Judy Jacques Ensemble on 28 August 2003,[8] and performances followed across the eastern states.

---

8   Jacques' strong suit of Doug de Vries, Sandro Donati, Nicola Eveleigh, Howard Cairns, Michael Jordan and Denis Close was supported on various tracks by Brian Brown, Tony Gould and Bob Sedergreen (see Jacques, 2005).

The singer had enjoyed her farm horses and vineyards for over 43 years. Fortuitously, she sold Wild Dog Hill in advance of its razing on 7 February 2009 during the worst bushfire in the nation's recorded history. Her plucky partner, the trumpeter Sandro Donati, saved lives and property in the St Andrews area, and produced the Montsalvat Black Saturday Recovery Benefit Concert in Eltham. In a sequence of cumulative change, Jacques had already purchased land at Killiecrankie, Flinders Island, to where the couple—still burdened by the deep loss of friends and their former farm—moved permanently in 2011.

Island Community Stardom

To what extent the singer's relocation to a secluded geographical locus has worked to obscure her long mainland career remains to be seen. However, the implication is that stardom affects, and in turn is affected by, an acute sense of place. A period of healing allowed Jacques to ground her stardom regionally through interaction with the Flinders Islanders (see Ryan, 2009) in small-scale musical contexts that are immediate and sustainable (e.g. variety nights and impromptu musical sessions).

As Pedelty (2012, p. 129) has remarked, it takes a great deal of work to cultivate ecologically meaningful musical relationships within a local community, and to this end Jacques has by no means 'rested on her laurels'. In partnership with Donati, her curation of the museum exhibition 'Celebrating the History of Music and Dance on the Furneaux Islands' (2013) entailed extensive research, musical instrument gathering and conversations partly focused around the search by local Indigenous peoples for security and self-determination. This productive attachment to island folk life reflects a view developed by Pedelty (2012) that the deceptively simple answer to the problem of unsustainable music is for all of us to start making more of it locally.

The power of music sometimes allows songs to outlive their original purpose, to find new meaning in new eras (Pedelty, 2012, p. 106), as was recently the case when Jacques' 1966 single reappeared in cyberspace.

Revived Northern Soul Stardom

In mid-2011, Niteowl Northern Soul Vids reactivated Jacques' cover version of 'You're Messin' Up My Mind'. In this clip, a set of archival still images captures the excitement of the Manchester nightclub scene, revealing more about the addictive subcultural movement than it does about Jacques. A promotion for the album *Club Soul Volume 2* spruiked the Northern Soul Revival: 'Go out and find a copy and play LOUD … take yourself back to those hallowed dancefloors, feel the hairs on the back of your neck tingle and drink in the atmosphere' (Scooter Geek on charly.co.uk, n.d.).

The canons of the movement's discrete repertoire were remarked in Australia by the Radio National broadcasters for *The Inside Sleeve*, who aired Jacques' single during an 'Obscure Australian "Northern Soul"' session on 1 February 2013 (ABC, 2013c). *RareCollections* subsequently presented the single in their sessions 'Northern Soul from Downunder' (ABC, 2013b) and 'Northern Soul' (ABC, 2014). Dismissed as having no commercial potential in Australia, 'You're Messin' Up My Mind' legitimised itself by taking root in the northern hemisphere, reappearing decades later in a revival movement and, in tandem with the latter development, rippling on in a heritage recording.

Heritage Stardom: *The Sixties Sessions*

Nathan Impiombato, producer of the specialist reissue label Playback Records, negotiated with Jacques in early 2015 to remaster her vinyl recordings. Channel 9's senior archivist listed approximately 20 of the singer's television performances, but could not easily access those on film (Nathan Impiombato, email to the author, 25 March 2016). Jacques provided a memory list of her shows on other networks; however, the heritage CD released on 17 October 2016 does not include bootleg recordings of live performances or television tracks from the era. Virtually all the songs make their CD-era debut: the studio recordings that Jacques made with The Yarra Yarra New Orleans Jazz Band and The Gospel Four; her solo work including the Northern Soul classic 'You're Messin' Up My Mind'; plus live tracks featuring Jacques on The Yarras' live LP—24 songs in total (Impiombato, email to the author, 15 November 2015).

4. 'YOU'RE MESSIN' UP MY MIND'

Playback Records website (2016) advertises 'the complete sixties recordings by Australia's Queen of Gospel and Trad Jazz', packaged with a retro cover (see Figure 4.4) and a 32-page booklet featuring rare and unpublished photos.

Figure 4.4: *Judy Jacques: The Sixties Sessions*. CD album cover
Source: Image courtesy Playback Records, 2016.

Summary: Shades of a Star That Has Not Yet Set

The application of the star metaphor to Judy Jacques' career has drawn out aspects of female gender in interplay with prevailing consumer taste. An internal precondition of talent saw the traction Jacques gained from an early position of musical promise hold firm until adult tension arose between her needs for public visibility and personal creativity. True to an early bent for female empowerment, personal wrests and turns saw Jacques eschew structured popular music orbits all for the delight of being free to sing 'herself'. Her career waxed and waned even as her imagination was freed and her vocal flexibility increased.

As manifested in other starscapes of sorts, that which is appreciated by one fan base may be anathema to another as an individual develops skills according to, against and beyond rigid models. In the negotiation between musical freedom and industry objectification, the determination of a star to evolve despite consumer taste is likely to be out of sync with the aesthetics dominating producers' decisions. It was Jacques' continual practice of singing across a lifetime that cohered the dismantling and reconstruction of her stardom. The patterns and tensions of change that the singer experienced between obligatory and emancipatory performance may be applicable, in varying inflections, to the careers of other performers. However, no single dominant paradigm can define the dynamic of a stardom in flux.

Acknowledgements

It is a pleasure to thank Judy Jacques for her correspondence and generous access to photographs. I am grateful to Nathan Impiombato for providing information on *The Sixties Sessions* and permission to reproduce the album cover. Thanks also to my anonymous referees, and to Dr Janice Newton for advice.

References

Australian Broadcasting Corporation. 2013a. 'Some of the Best Pressed for Crest'. *RareCollections*, 26 May 2013. abc.net.au/radionational/programs/rarecollections/crest/4705524 (accessed 25 March 2016).

———. 2013b. 'Northern Soul from Downunder'. *RareCollections*, 3 February 2013. abc.net.au/radionational/programs/rarecollections/northern-soul-fromdownunder/4494086 (accessed 25 March 2016).

———. 2013c. 'Obscure Australian "Northern Soul" & Melbourne's Ainslie Wills'. *The Inside Sleeve*, 1 February 2013. abc.net.au/radionational/programs/insidesleeve/ise-1-02-2013/4496468 (accessed 25 March 2016).

———. 2014. 'Northern Soul'. *RareCollections*, 7 December 2014. abc.net.au/radionational/programs/rarecollections/the-northernsoul/5906522 (accessed 25 March 2016).

Bartlett, M. 2015. 'Georgy Girl: The Seekers Musical'. *The Weekly Review*, 25 November, 15.

Brown, E. J. n.d. '50 Years of the Yarra Yarra Jazz Band'. The Eric Brown Collection, Australian Jazz Archives. vicjazzarchive.org.au/6jazznews2.htm (accessed 25 March 2016).

Charly.co.uk. n.d. 'Various Artists: *Club Soul Volume 2—The Twisted Wheel*'. charly.co.uk/albums/club-soul-volume-2-the-twisted-wheel/ (accessed 17 November 2015).

Frith, S. 1996. *Performing Rites: On the Value of Popular Music*. Oxford: Oxford University Press.

Jacques, J. 2005. 'Passing the Torch: Commemorating the Songs of Fanny Cochrane Smith'. In *Popular Music: Commemoration, Commodification and Communication: Proceedings of the 2004 IASPM Australia New Zealand Conference, Held in Conjunction with the Symposium of the International Musicological Society, 11–16 July, 2004*, edited by D. Crowdy, 11–19. International Association for the Study of Popular Music, Australia and New Zealand Branch.

Johnson, B. 1987. 'Judy Jacques'. In *The Oxford Companion to Australian Jazz*, 58. Melbourne: Oxford University Press.

King, A. R. 1980. 'Innovation, Creativity, and Performance'. In *The Ethnography of Musical Performance*, edited by M. Herndon and N. McLeod, 167–75. Norwood, PA: Norwood Editions.

McLeod, N. and M. Herndon. 1980. 'Conclusion'. In *The Ethnography of Musical Performance*, edited by M. Herndon and N. McLeod, 176–199. Norwood, PA: Norwood Editions.

Negus, K. 1995. 'Where the Mystical Meets the Market: Creativity and Commerce in the Production of Popular Music'. *Sociological Review* 43 (2): 316–341. doi.org/10.1111/j.1467-954X.1995.tb00606.x

Pedelty, M. 2012. *Ecomusicology: Rock, Folk, and the Environment.* Philadelphia: Temple University Press.

Pidd, H. 2012. 'Twisted Wheel joins Cavern and Wigan Casino in Music Venue Graveyard'. *The Guardian*, 28 December www.theguardian.com/music/2012/dec/27/twisted-wheel-northern-soul-venue-manchester (accessed 17 November 2015).

Playback Records. 2016. 'Playback Records Recondite Reissues'. playbackrecords.net (accessed 17 October 2016).

Ryan, R. 2009. 'Modelling Compositional Artistry for Musical Understanding: Judy Jacques and the Flinders Island Community'. In *Musical Understanding: Proceedings of the Australian Society for Music Education XVII National Conference*, edited by W. Baker, 182–91. Launceston: Australian Society for Music Education.

——. 2014. 'Judy Jacques, Jazz, and the Sheer Joy of Singing: A 70th Birthday Tribute'. *Jazzline* 47 (2): 3–15.

Sharpe, J. 2008. *I Wanted to be a Jazz Musician.* Canberra: National Film and Sound Archive.

Whiteoak, J. 2008. 'Improvisation and Popular Music'. In *Sounds of Then, Sounds of Now: Popular Music in Australia*, edited by Shane Homan and Tony Mitchell, 37–60. University of Tasmania, Hobart: ACYS Publishing.

Audiovisual References

Bandstand. 1955–66. *The Best of Bandstand.* DVD Collection. Volume 3: *Live at the Myer Music Bowl in March 1965.* Melbourne: Umbrella label.

Brown, B. 1987. *Winged Messenger: Brian Brown Quartet with Judy Jacques.* Melbourne: Aija Recordings [Vinyl LP].

Jacques, J. 1963. *Judy Jacques and Her Gospel Four.* Melbourne: Crest Records [EP].

———. 1964. *Be My Friend: Judy Jacques and Her Gospel Four*. Melbourne: Segue [EP].

———. 1966. *You're Messin' Up My Mind*. Melbourne: Astor [45 rpm single].

———. 1997. *Going for a Song: Judy Jacques and Lighthouse*. St Andrews, Victoria: Wild Dog Hill Studio [CD].

———. 2002. *Making Wings*. The Judy Jacques Ensemble. St Andrews, Victoria: Wild Dog Hill Studio [CD].

Niteowl Northern Soul Vids. 2011. *Judy Jacques—Messing Up My Mind—Northern Soul*. Uploaded July 3. youtube.com/watch?v=t9JDZ5DJ-K0 (accessed 25 March 2016).

Playback Records. 2016. *Judy Jacques: The Sixties Sessions*. Featuring The Yarra Yarra New Orleans Jazz Band and The Gospel Four. Produced by Nathan Impiombato, Geelong, Victoria. CD-004.

Yarra Yarra New Orleans Jazz Band. 1962a. *Yarra Yarra New Orleans Jazz Band with Judy Jacques*, Vol. I. Melbourne: Crest Records [EP].

———. 1962b. *Yarra Yarra New Orleans Jazz Band with Judy Jacques*, Vol. 2. Melbourne: Crest Records [EP].

———. 1963. *Jazz as You Like It. The Yarra Yarra Jazz Band Featuring Judy Jacques*. Melbourne: Crest Records [live LP recorded at City Hall].

———. 1994. *The Yarra Yarra Reunion Band Featuring Judy Jacques*. Melbourne: Newmarket [CD].

5

Wendy Saddington: Beyond an 'Underground Icon'

Julie Rickwood

> [Wendy Saddington] sung with a gutsiness that no other chick singer in Australia even approached … There would be few singers from overseas that could match her, and everyone soon knew it … Wendy was the star of the [East Coast Rock] festival (Elfick, 1970, cited in McFarlane, 2011).

Introduction

After Wendy Saddington passed away in March 2013 at the age of 63, an outpouring of grief, recollection and admiration for her unique contribution to Australian popular music erupted on her Facebook page and in the media (see McFarlane, 2013; Brown, 2013; Watts, 2013).

'Saddington had attitude', Everett True said in 2015. Loene Carmen (2012) had previously announced that Saddington had 'this utterly unique gift of a heart-stopping old soul singer's voice and fully-formed, almost punk fuck-you, performance aesthetic'. Kathleen Stewart (2006) declared, 'I loved ballsy women singers like her, with more vocal passion and range than was fashionable in the early eighties'.

So, if you heard someone declaring that '[s]he was amazing, such an icon and fiercely pioneering artist, paving the way for the rest of us female musicians' (Levin, 2013), you might be forgiven for thinking they were further describing Wendy Saddington. That description was actually applied to Chrissy Amphlett, lead singer of the Divinyls, after she also passed away in 2013. Similar comments have also been made about Saddington's friend and sometimes collaborator Renée Geyer, who recognised Saddington's equal ability to '[tear] up the mike' (Stratton, 2008, p. 183)

It is not unexpected that Amphlett's legacy to Australian popular music is greater than Saddington's, given Amphlett's profile in recorded music and the mainstream Australian rock industry generally. Nevertheless, many of the statements about Amphlett's pioneering role for Australian women musicians eclipse Saddington's equally 'pioneering' role. In fact, Amphlett is among many who have cited Saddington as an influence. Others include Robert Forster of the Go-Betweens, actress/singer Loene Carmen and Karise Eden, winner of *The Voice* in 2012 (True, 2015; Bayly, 2015).

The high praise given to the musical legacies of both women was, nevertheless, unusual. It happens infrequently, despite women having always contributed to various genres of music making in Australia (for example, see Barrand, 2010). The contributions of women to Australian popular music in the past have been poorly celebrated or documented. Further, women musicians remain hidden or underrepresented, as an analysis of Triple J's 2016 Hottest 100 reveals (Riley, 2016) and as has been previously noted in academic discourse (Strong, 2010). An article on the Icon exhibition 'Rock Chicks' declared in its opening line that any search engine would contain very little of relevance to Australian women in rock music history and observed the 'sad lack of notetaking on the influence of female musicians … in Australian rock history' (*Beat Magazine*, 2010). Whiteley (2013, p. 83) highlighted that to ignore gender inequality in popular music is a failure of popular music studies. More recently, Strong (2015, p. 150) argued:

> The lack of information that we have about past female rockers makes it harder for women in Australia to see this field as one they can participate in, and also makes the retention of memories about currently successful women musicians less likely. This leads to a situation where documenting information about these women should be an imperative for popular music scholars.

5. WENDY SADDINGTON

Figure 5.1: Wendy Saddington, Station Hotel Melbourne, 1976
Source: Courtesy of Peter Maloney.

Therefore, this chapter goes some way in documenting information about Wendy Saddington, whose contribution to Australian popular music is understudied. It draws from various sources: music journalists, commentators, fans and, importantly, an exhibition at Canberra Museum and Gallery (CMAG) that opened during the IASPM–ANZ Branch Popular Music, Stars and Stardom Conference in Canberra in December 2015. The chapter explores the documentation and commentary that surrounded Saddington's career during her life and posthumously. It addresses the lack of attention given to her work through the lens of Australian popular music and gender, especially the expectations and treatment of women musicians by the Australian rock industry in the 1970s.[1]

Australian Popular Music in the 1970s

> No, we are not freaks, we are human beings grasping at a freedom. (Saddington 1970)

By the early 1970s, young popular music audiences in Australia sought 'direction and identity in alternative patterns of social interaction, in fashion and the arts; some of them also began to develop distinctive political outlooks and dabbled with alternative economic theories' (Douglas and Geeves, 1992, p. 101). The Vietnam War, sexual liberation, women's liberation, the election of Prime Minister Gough Whitlam and a wider sense of values and preferences that included rock music had introduced an alternative culture. As Douglas and Geeves (1992, p. 103) suggest, 'many ... genuinely believed they stood at the "dawning of the age of Aquarius" and on the brink of revolution'. In the late 1960s Wendy Saddington was embedded in the psychedelic era with friends and colleagues in the music and art worlds (for example, see McIntyre, 2006a, 2006b; Leatherdale, 2014). As the quote above indicates, she was firmly placed in that social and cultural change, almost anticipating the 'countercultural wave of the coming years' (McIntyre, 2006b, p. 188).

Those investing in these new ways of being were students, hippies and rock fans looking for more in contemporary music and lyrics than was offered by the established Australian recording industry, radio stations and television programs. They were understood as rejecting mindless pop or teeny-bopper music, instead consuming various subgenres of rock music that included soul, blues, heavy rock, acid rock, jazz rock, country rock and folk rock (Douglas and Geeves, 1992, p. 105; McIntyre, 2006a). This 'underground' music was given intellectual analysis by those rejecting pop, which brought a respectability to those within it.

---

1 Since writing this chapter, the *Journal of World Popular Music* has dedicated a volume to 'Gender, Popular Music and Australian Identity' (2016, 3[1]), which expands many of the arguments made here.

5. WENDY SADDINGTON

According to Marks (2006), the early 1970s were years of diversity in Australian popular music, with an accepted division between 'progressive rock' musicians such as Skyhooks, Daddy Cool, Billy Thorpe and the Aztecs, Lah De Dahs, Chain, Zoot, Max Merritt and the Meteors, Jeff St John, Copperwine, Axiom, and the 'bubblegum' contingent such as Johnny Farnham and John Paul Young. The most significant feature within this representation of 'progressive rock' is the absence of any direct reference to women musicians. It was only male musicians who were promoted as 'finally singing directly to Australians in a language they understood' (Douglas and Geeves, 1992, p. 107). As Douglas and Geeves recognised, while the feminist movement had some impact on Australian society, the 'rock music business remained unremittingly chauvinist' (1992, p. 107). Among the few women musicians at the time, the 'only woman performer given enthusiastic and serious attention was Wendy Saddington' (Douglas and Geeves, 1992, p. 107).

While recognising Saddington's contribution to Australian popular music in the 1970s, it must be recognised that she was not the only female rock musician during the 1970s to early 1980s. Contemporaries included Margret RoadKnight, Jeannie Little, Linda George, Renée Geyer and the female members of Stiletto. These women were removed from the 'limp queens of pop like Alison Durbin and Olivia Newton-John and a few "personalities" like Denise Drysdale, who were not taken seriously as musicians'[2] (Douglas and Geeves, 1992, p. 107).

Saddington was a pioneer in the rock music scene in the late 1960s. McFarlane (2011) noted that during the grip of the pop 'scream scene' in Australia, Chain, which featured Saddington, was one of the 'first local bands with a progressive outlook, and by the end of [1969] the underground Melbourne scene was beginning to burgeon forth'. By this time, Saddington had already been named 'The Face of '68' by *Go-Set*, the Australian pop magazine of the 1960s and 1970s,[3] describing her as 'singing like a white Aretha Franklin, loud, raucous, soulful and gutsy' (*Go-Set*, 1968), and had fronted blues/psych band The Revolution and psych-pop band James Taylor Move. She was similar to other 'blue-eyed soul' singers, drawing on Motown soul and blues for her musical

---

2 As Strong (2015) has noted, this dismissal of pop music as disposable and not requiring talent reinforces the wider social hierarchies between men and women. See also Nelligan (2016).
3 *Go-Set* celebrated its 50th anniversary with an interactive website: smh.com.au/interactive/2016/school-of-pop/

expression. Many commentators at the time likened her to Janis Joplin, a comparison she did not enjoy. While acknowledging that it was 'a compliment I suppose', she added that 'Janis was the great white hope and it killed her ... I'm no great white hope. I'm an out-of-money, frizzy-haired singer greatly influenced by the styles of Aretha Franklin and Nina Simone' (quoted in Nimmervoll, 1971, p. 10). McIntyre (2006b, p. 187) claimed that 'Wendy was so distinctive in her presentation of her personal life and her music that she had developed a cult following'. She was at the cutting edge of alternative music making and possessed the capacity to move from band to band, driven by a desire to find musicians who could support her unique voice with empathetic professionalism and similar aesthetic and artistic aspirations.

An Outline of Saddington's Career

Most commentators limit Saddington's recording output to the single 'Looking Through a Window' (1971) and the CD of her live performance with the Copperwine at The Odyssey Music Festival (1971, 1972). The release of the live performance recording was against Saddington's wishes, as it was never intended to be a commercial release. These two recordings were re-released as a compilation by Aztec Music in 2011.

Additional recordings that capture her voice have, however, been produced. Saddington recorded three tracks on the 1984 Hare Krishna Band CD *Where to Now?*. Her performance of Bob Marley's 'Redemption Song' on that recording was described as a 'glorious version' (McFarlane, 2011). She did backing vocals on the Kevin Borich Express CD *One Night Jamm*, recorded three tracks on the *Women 'n Blues* CD in 2003, and was included on the *Soulful Sisters: From the 60s and 70s* CD in 2013 with the track 'Looking Through A Window' and *Then & Now: Australia Salutes the Beatles* CD in 2014 with the track 'Tomorrow Never Knows', both of which were from her earlier recordings. Other attempts were made to record her voice but all failed due to technical or other issues (see McFarlane, 2011; Culnane, 2008). Her recordings, however, do not fully document her contribution to Australian popular music.

Saddington featured on music television shows such as *Fusion*, *Radio with Pictures* and *GTK*, including a half-hour special screened as *Wendy Saddington and Friends* on 24 and 31 January 1973. This special also featured Jeff St John and Morris Spinetti (aka Teardrop) and revealed her striking clown-inspired performance persona. She also featured in Peter Weir's 1972 film *3 Directions in Australian Pop Music* with a similar performance. Her heartfelt rendition of 'I Think of You'[4] in this film is significantly different from the Captain Matchbox Whoppee Band's comic act and the psychedelic nature of Indelible Murtcepts.[5] Saddington was the sole female performer featured in the episode 'Billy Killed the Fish 1968–1973' in the *Long Way to the Top* series: coverage that was brief and poorly articulated. Later, the series was criticised for its male-centric nature (Strong, 2015, p. 151). In 2012, Saddington appeared on the Special Broadcasting Service (SBS) program *RocKwiz*, performing 'Backlash Blues', a long-performed cover of a Nina Simone classic.

Chronologically, Saddington's live performance career can be mapped over five decades, across numerous music venues, especially in Melbourne, Sydney and Canberra. Her performances were prolific and have been significantly outlined by McFarlane (2011) in his notes accompanying the re-release of her two major recordings. Her festival appearances were during the height of her popularity: The Odyssey at Wallacia, New South Wales (NSW) (1971), The Myponga Festival of Progressive Music, South Australia (1971), The Pilgrimage for Pop, NSW (1970), East Coast Rock Festival in Sydney (1970), and the Miracle Festival in rural Victoria (1970).

Influenced by Nina Simone, Aretha Franklin, Mahalia Jackson and other blues singers and US soul music (McFarlane, 2013), Saddington's musical preferences are telling. She mostly sang covers or songs penned by others for her. These were songs that were message driven, supporting her political and social leanings. Her ambition was to record her own songs, although she was far from a prolific songwriter. Her song 'Five People Know I'm Crazy' and 'Blues in A' were the only ones recorded; however, she also performed others including 'I Want to go Home', a song she wrote in New York when she was able to devote time to writing lyrics. MacLean (1972) described the numerous song lyrics written in New York as 'almost overwhelmingly expressive, and each one had a point made clear in beautiful style' but needy of the empathetic hand of a composer to come to fruition. By 1973, she had 'drifted and generally progressed further into her one-woman repertoire of songs' and even 'spontaneous, improvised, free-form music that [was] developed between Wendy and

---

4   A cover of cult US folk singer/songwriter Sixto Rodriguez (McFarlane, 2013).
5   The Indelible Murtcepts was the alter ego of the band Spectrum.

her accompanying musicians' (Nugent, 1973). 'Blues in A' was an ideal vehicle for improvisation and performances of the song were very fluid (Maloney, 2016). Saddington also wrote a song for Billy Thorpe, 'Mothers and Fathers', which was recorded on the *Thump'n Pig & Puff'n Billy—Downunda* recording in 1973, and later re-released as a CD in 2005.[6]

Part of her desire to travel to the US in 1971 was to find musicians and a music industry that could support her appropriately. She ventured overseas to discover other possibilities because she had 'sung everywhere [she] could in Australia' (*Go-Set*, 1971). The brief stay did not deliver the professional experiences she was hoping for, but it exposed her to other influences. Especially notable was the theatrical attire that emerged on her return to Australia, having lived with performance artist Jeff Crozier in his 'tool shed' in New York (MacLean, 1972). These theatrical performances could '[bewilder] sections of the audience [who were not] accustomed to an artist releasing so much emotion' (Nugent, 1972).

Saddington's motivation to sing was to 'make more people cry and feel things' (MacLean, 1971b), but she was repeatedly disappointed with the skills of bands she joined willingly and bands supplied by venues. She tired of the demands of daily performances and poor payment. Recording promises rarely materialised. 'People just don't understand you or recognise what you do' she declared in 1971 (MacLean, 1971a).

Saddington also contributed to the popular music scene through her work with *Go-Set*. The weekly magazine was the first to explore 'an emerging and developing Australian popular music industry' (Kent, 1998, p. 1; see also McIntyre, 2006a). As a writer, she was both music journalist and 'agony aunt'. Her entry into journalism was featured on the cover of the September 1969 edition. Her advice column, 'Wendy Saddington takes care of business', dealt with the reality of teenagers' problems directly and, at times, controversially. Her responses were far from conservative. Saddington's full-page image also featured in May 1970 above the headline 'Go-Set says goodbye to Wendy'. She was well aware of bias in the rock industry, stating:

---

6   Most songs were written by Billy Thorpe and Warren Morgan, who, together with other legendary musicians, recorded this album. Additional live tracks were added to the CD re-release in 2005 (see Vogt, 2005; McFarlane, 2011).

> Go-Set doesn't give enough space to good unknown people. It talks about the same ones over and over—like Russell Morris and Johnny Farnham, and if anyone else goes along to places like Uptight, they're treated like dirt. You have to belong to the in group, or you're considered to be just crap. (Samantha, 1969)

Eventually, she proceeded 'to shun the rock world and its endless promotion as a hollow and ultimately futile exercise' (Bayly, 2015), performing outside the 'high bracket rock scene' (Nugent, 1973) throughout the 1980s and 1990s.

Australian Popular Music and Saddington

Richard Guilliatt (2012) recognised the deeply masculine influence on Australian music in the 1970s in his contribution to *The Monthly* entitled 'That Blockhead Thing'. Concentrating on Billy Thorpe and the Aztecs, he cited music journalist Murray Engleheart's description of Australian popular music at the time, 'Blood, Sweat and Beers', as an apt label for bands such as the Aztecs that 'kept both feet planted in blues machismo while astral travelling' (Guilliatt, 2012). He stated:

> The only chicks in sight are wearing 'Band Moll' T-shirts. Sunbury famously featured only one female performer in its first three years, the extraordinary Wendy Saddington, an Afro-haired blues shouter who appeared at the 1972 festival after recording her one and only album, then retreated from the scene. It wasn't a time for anyone who had trouble dealing with the male id. (p. 59)

Guilliatt's statement begs investigation. It reinforces what Strong (2015, p. 150) has argued is the 'symbolic alignment between men and rock in the collective memory of Australian music'. It places women distinctly as sexualised audience, is somewhat insulting to Saddington's musicianship by reducing her to simply a 'shouter' and suggests the male id as the reason for her withdrawal from public performance.

Sunbury, a music festival on the outskirts of Melbourne that began in 1972, signalled a shift away from the music inspired by the 1960s hippie ethos to the grittier sounds of pub rock (Arts Centre Melbourne, n.d.). Billy Thorpe and the Aztecs were on that first stage, as was Chain, but without Saddington.

Interestingly, Warren Morgan, a member of Chain and later the Aztecs, wrote songs and instrumentally supported Saddington in her only recorded single. Chain and the Aztecs were not the only male musicians to collaborate with Saddington in recordings and live performances. As outlined above, Saddington also recorded with Copperwine, the Hare Krishna Band and the Kevin Borich Express, and performed with The Revolution and James Taylor Move. These same musicians and others performed as members of her backing bands in live performances. She also shared the stage with Ross Wilson, Barry McAskill, Lobby Lloyd and Max Merritt. She performed in the rock opera *Tommy*, alongside Daryl Braithwaite, Billy Thorpe, Broderick Smith and Keith Moon. The Wendy Saddington Band, which performed in the early 1980s, featured jazz pianist Bobby Gebert, guitarist Harvey James, bass guitarist Billy Rylands and drummer Chris Sweeney; the later line-up included Mick Liber and Des McKenna. Her later performances were most often with rock pianist and singer-songwriter Peter Head.

This suggests that rather than having 'trouble dealing with the male id', Saddington's musicianship was highly valued by her male cohort. Her voice was greatly acknowledged by music journalists, including Molly Meldrum, who declared 'her voice is unbelievable … to compare it with any other would be a criminal act' (Meldrum, 1968). Interestingly, while Meldrum obviously admired Saddington's voice and worked with her at *Go-Set*, she never appeared on *Countdown*, possibly because, as is discussed below, she did not fulfil the standard requirements of female musicians, especially for television. Further, it may also be because of her later withdrawal from mainstream performances. Not unexpectedly then, Saddington was absent from the *Molly* miniseries. Only three female Australian artists appear across the soundtrack discs: Kylie Minogue, Tina Arena and Chrissy Amphlett, with the Divinyls. This selection not only reinforces what constitutes mainstream acceptance and thereby memory of Australian popular music, but, as Strong (2016, p. 2) articulates, the program and its soundtrack again raise the question 'about the extent to which only white men will be presented as important to popular music in Australia'.

Other journalists at the time similarly pronounced Saddington as 'the best female rhythm-and-blues singer in this country' (Raffaele, 1969), and 'a star, she's a star' (*Go-Set*, 1971). Nugent (1973) not only acknowledged her as 'the finest female feel [sic] singer in Australia' but firmly placed her in the rock scene. Her influence on other women singers was also articulated because of the passion, raw intensity and power of her voice (Peter Head, quoted in Watts, 2013, p. 12). Her long-time friend and musical collaborator Jeff St John (2013) shared a memory in his eulogy for her:

> It seems that she was just suddenly there and I was happily sharing the stage with one of the most electrifying voices and personalities I have ever been graced to know. Her commitment to a song was total and absolute. Her understanding and empathy for a lyric was second to none, whether you, as a listener, grasped the song or not, she'd touch your soul. Such was the power of this gifted, enigmatic woman.

Beyond the Music

> Wendy Saddington's trademark kohled eyes, pale, sombre lips and enormous Afro suited her wildcat purr and other-worldly rhythm-and-blues improvisations. On her small but powerful frame, singlets, vests, Levis and lashings of gypsy jewellery defied the 'girly' look then expected of the tiny percentage of females who managed to fight their way into the spotlight. (Brown, 2013)

> By Wendy Saddington's own admission, she could be at times a somewhat confrontational, stubborn and terrifying prospect for audiences, friends and enemies—a fact that was to both help and hinder her musical career. (McIntyre, 2006b)

The privileging of white male Australian musicians reinforces an attitude that devalues female musicians in subtle ways, particularly regarding physical appearances. Saddington could be described as frail and little (see Meldrum, 1968), but her strong performances and compelling presence were often also mentioned. This tension was frequently noted. She was introduced to *Go-Set* readers as 'a little girl with a pixie face and a big voice and lots of hair, and some call her tough' (Samantha, 1969).

Wendy Saddington challenged the popular music industry. As with most female musicians, her looks and style drew frequent comment, although they focused on her unconventional appearance. She was 'strange looking' (*Go-Set*, 1968), 'tough, sensitive, vulgar and shy' (Caught in the Act 1970, cited in McIntyre, 2006b), she broke 'all the rules … drinking, smoking and swearing on stage' (Stoves, 1971). This was also admired, as Chlopicki (2011) later recognised:

She looked like a cross between The Bellrays' Lisa Kekaula and Germaine Greer—photographs of her exude independence and an earthy kind of cool; you can bet there would have been hordes of girls wandering around Darlinghurst and Fitzroy in 1970 whose entire look was based on Saddington. Not that such physical concerns were Wendy's bag.

Photographs capture her often intense presence. Greg Weight's portrait of Saddington with Chain (1969) is part of the National Library of Australia Collection. Saddington's 1973 portrait by feminist photographer Carol Jerrems is part of the collection at the National Gallery of Australia. In August 1994, Australian art historian Catriona Moore dedicated her book, *Indecent Exposures. Twenty Years of Australian Feminist Photography* (1994) to Jerrems and used Saddington's photograph to promote the work, as did Helen Ennis in her review of the book (Ennis, 1994). Mark Juddery's (2006) article 'Almost Famous' also used a portrait of Saddington as its leading image. Other images of Saddington were taken by John Newhill, Peter Maloney and Brett Hilder; many were captured by Phillip Morris.

Saddington might have been petite with striking features but, more importantly, she was a musician who expected professionalism from those around her. While she could not necessarily articulate it, she knew what she wanted and recognised its lack in many of the musicians with whom she worked. Saddington said that 'all the bands I've had I've never been on the same wavelength musically. I know inside me what I want to do, but I don't know how to say it, to them' (Frazer, 1970). She was 'definitely her own woman and [wouldn't] be pushed into something she [didn't] want to do' (MacLean, 1971a).

Saddington's independence and strong convictions were notable in other ways. True (2015) argued she was a 'feminist icon', possibly because of her outspoken statements in her role at *Go-Set* on issues such as pregnancy, loneliness and drug addiction (Kent, 1998; McIntyre, 2006a), her connections with lesbian and feminist creatives (e.g. see McIntyre, 2006a) and her support of the Sydney-based libertarian collective Sylvia and the Synthetics during the formative years of the Australian Gay Rights movement (True, 2015). She was certainly involved in feminist and counterculture movements, and strongly opposed the Vietnam War (e.g. see Saddington, 1970; Stoves, 1971). Jeff St John described her as a 'champion of causes' (cited in Brown, 2013). It has been suggested that Saddington fended off sexual approaches by men (Brown, 2013; Maloney,

2016), identified as lesbian (Brown, 2013; Maloney, 2015) and, after she joined the Hare Krishna movement, as confirmed by those close to her, was celibate (McFarlane, 2011; Maloney, 2015; Bayly, 2015). Therefore, her sexual identity was fluid.

Saddington's independence, outspokenness and assertive (at times acerbic) nature often featured in reviews or interviews. In some interviews, she was deliberately provocative. Just as easily as she could capture and mesmerise her audiences, she could also leave them unsatisfied and disgruntled. She would walk out of gigs, upset with the supporting musicians or the venue conditions. McFarlane (2011) described her as 'a mess of contradiction and not an easy persona for the public at large to accept'.

Her relationships with other musicians could also be difficult, as suggested by her frequent changes of bands due to musical differences and divergent paths. Phil Manning stated that 'working with Wendy was quite an incredible experience, and although it was fun at times, we wouldn't wish to go through it again' (Elfick, 1969, cited in McFarlane, 2011). Years later, Peter Head acknowledged that working with Saddington was unpredictable. 'Sometimes it was great; sometimes it could end in some kind of disaster, but most of the time, musically it was great' (quoted in Watts, 2013, p. 2). These narratives and similar others are overwhelmingly from men. However, as previously articulated, many musicians, both male and female, acknowledge her complexity, but, importantly, they highlight her influence on their musical careers.

She challenged and had difficulty with the 'cut-throat world of corporate rock' and would 'shrink back and depart from the scene … almost as if success was anathema to her' (McFarlane, 2013). Jeff St John (2013, cited in Bayly, 2015) said her withdrawals resulted from a disillusionment with the music industry more than anything else. Saddington certainly 'tired of the pettiness of the music business and embraced spirituality through conversion to the Hare Krishna faith' (Curran, 2011), a part of her life I do not engage with in any detail in this chapter.

The 'Underground Icon' Exhibition

The 'Underground Icon' exhibition at the CMAG in 2015–16 was the first exhibition dedicated solely to the career of one female Australian musician. It was a significant contribution to maintaining Saddington's legacy in cultural history and collective memory. Exhibitions at the Arts Centre Melbourne had featured women musicians; however, 'Kylie Minogue: The Costume Collection' focused on fashion and identity, and 'Rock Chicks' featured many other musicians but not Wendy Saddington.

'Underground Icon' was made possible because of the remarkable admiration for Saddington held by the collector of much of the archival material included, visual artist Peter Maloney, and the curator of the exhibition, his partner, Mark Bayly. Maloney is also one of the administrators of the Wendy Saddington Facebook page, which further captures the memories and recollections of her friends and fans.

Maloney first saw Saddington perform when he was about 17 years old; he 'was transfixed by the experience … led willingly on a journey into a cultural underground' (Bayly, 2015). Saddington continued to be a fascination for Maloney and he became devoted to her and her career. 'The two met by chance in the streets of Sydney's Darlinghurst in the late 1980s when he was resident there' (Bayly, 2015). By this time, Maloney had lost virtually his entire circle of friends in the city to HIV/AIDS and the two artists developed a lasting friendship.

Maloney and Bayly used a variety of objects and sources: photographs, posters, sound recordings, reviews, interviews, film clips, paintings and personal memorabilia, including postcards Maloney received from Saddington. The film clips played in a continuous loop, saturating the exhibition space with Saddington's unique voice and style. Other recorded material was accessed through headphones. In addition to Maloney's archival collection, the exhibition included works sourced from the ABC, the National Gallery of Australia, the National Library of Australia and other private collections. This variety of objects and sources produced a memorial that revisited her achievements and captured personal moments and her connection with others.

Very little of her spiritual life was mentioned in the exhibition. Instead, it concentrated on celebrating Saddington and her musical career. It did not consider the perplexing notion of why she was not successful in the mainstream music industry, but rather highlighted her talents and achievements. Involved in the floor talk given by Peter Maloney and, as discussions with museum staff verified, I was well aware that people were captivated by the exhibition. It was an immersive environment utilising visual and aural cues that became 'animated by way of … memories and the affect generated' (Baker, Istvandity and Nowak, 2016, p. 77).

Conclusion

> [M]any people are agreeing that Wendy Saddington is the most unique talent Australia has ever produced. (MacLean, 1971a)

> She's the real thing, as honest, brutal, haunting and pure a songstress as Australia has ever had the honour of laying claim to. (Carmen, 2012)

In 1968, *Go-Set* declared Wendy Saddington the face of Australian music. During the early 1970s, she wrote for the magazine and reviews of her performances and interviews were frequent. She also featured in other magazines such as *Sound Blast, Music Maker, Weekender, Gas* and *Daily Planet*. She graced the front cover of the first edition of *Magazine* in February 1970. Her death in 2013 prompted an outpouring of grief, recollection and admiration, which continues on her administered Facebook page. In 2015, Gayle Austin played Saddington's 'Looking Through a Window' as the opening track in Double J and Triple J's 40th anniversary celebration. Later that year, the first exhibition dedicated solely to the career of one woman in Australian popular music was opened in her honour. In the decades between, Wendy Saddington performed in numerous venues and at festivals, was heard on radio and watched on television. Her live performances were many and most often outstanding. Called the 'undisputed Queen of Soul' (Frazer, 1970), 'Australia's Lady of Soul' or 'First Lady of the Blues' (McFarlane, 2013), it is to Australia's detriment that she was supported so ineffectually by the mainstream popular music industry. Saddington is said to have stated she was 'not into legacies' (Schwartz, 2012) and Peter Head declared that 'she didn't *want* to get famous' (cited in Watts, 2013, emphasis in original), but, as this investigation reveals, Wendy Saddington is an important musician in Australian popular music history.

Saddington has been described as 'mercurial', her early career 'meteoric', her later performances occurring 'once in a blue moon' and her spiritual path into Krishna Consciousness might be described as 'transcendent'. These are delightfully applicable metaphors for the theme of popular music, stars and stardom. More significantly, they aptly describe a complex individual in a challenging industry: an industry that could not find a way to work with Saddington in a way that truly recognised her individual and unique talent but rather assessed her from its own problematic and biased perspective. As MacLean (1971a) assessed, she was an 'over-publicised, underexposed super-talent'. Too often Saddington's personality was blamed for her lack of success rather than the systemic inequalities that existed in the 1970s. That hypermasculine rock industry had little capacity to encourage and support a woman of non-heteronormative sexuality with an unusual talent. Such a musician was simply not encouraged by the industry and her contribution has subsequently been neglected. Had the industry treated her differently, she might have indeed become a well-known 'star' and her talent given greater recognition than even the complimentary 'underground icon' delivers.

Acknowledgements

Thank you to Peter Maloney and Mark Bayly for granting access to the collection in the 'Wendy Saddington: Underground Icon' exhibition. I would also like to give a note of gratitude to the reviewers of the previous versions of this chapter for their supportive and constructive critique.

References

Arts Centre Melbourne. n.d. 'Sunbury'. collections.artscentremelbourne.com.au/#details=ecatalogue.39576 (accessed 2 February 2016).

Baker, S., L. Istvandity and R. Nowak. 2016. 'The Sound of Music Heritage: Curating Popular Music in Music Museums and Exhibitions'. *International Journal of Heritage Studies* 22 (1): 70–81. doi.org/10.1080/13527258.2015.1095784

Barrand, J. 2010. 'Rock Chicks: Women in Australia Music'. Melbourne: Victoria Arts Trust, 6 November 2010 – 27 February 2011.

Bayly, M. 2015. 'Wendy Saddington: Underground Icon'. Canberra: CMAG, December 2015 – June 2016.

Beat Magazine. 2010. 'Rock Chicks'. beat.com.au/content/rock-chicks (accessed 2 February 2016).

Brown, J. J. 2013. '"Electrifying" Melbourne Singer Who Swam Against the Tide of Pop'. *Sydney Morning Herald*, 9 July. smh.com.au/comment/obituaries/electrifying-melbourne-singer-who-swam-against-the-tide-of-pop-20130708-2pmbr.html (accessed 10 February 2015).

Carmen, L. 2012. 'Wendy Saddington and Peter Head @ Camelot Lounge, Marrickville, Sydney, 29.04.12'. *Collapse Board.* collapseboard.com/reviews/live-reviews/wendy-saddington-and-peter-head-camelot-lounge-marrickville-sydney-29-04-12/ (accessed 10 February 2015).

Chlopicki, I. T. 2011. 'Wendy Saddington—Five People Said I'm Crazy'. *Mess+Noise: An Australian Music Magazine.* messandnoise.com/releases/2000943 (accessed 2 February 2016).

Culnane, P. 2008. 'Wendy Saddington'. *Milesago.* milesago.com/artists/saddington.htm (accessed 10 February 2015).

Curran, A. 2011. 'Live'. *Mess+Noise: An Australian Music Magazine* messandnoise.com/releases/2000943 (accessed 10 February 2015).

Douglas, L. and R. Geeves. 1992. 'Music, Counter-Culture and the Vietnam Era'. In *From Pop to Punk to Postmodernism: Popular Music and Australian Culture from the 1960s to the 1990s*, edited by Philip Hayward, 101–112. North Sydney: Allen & Unwin.

Ennis, H. 1994. 'Review of Indecent Exposures: Twenty Years of Australian Feminist Photography. Catriona Moore'. *Canberra Times*, 23 August, 8.

Frazer, P. 1970. 'Wendy's Blues'. *Revolution*, 1 May – 1 June, 15.

Geyer, R. with E. Nimmervoll. 2000. *Confessions of a Difficult Woman: The Renée Geyer Story*. Pymble, NSW: Harper Collins.

Go-Set. 1968. 'The Face of '68'. 3 July, 12.

———. 1970. 'Go-Set Says Goodbye to Wendy'. 9 May, 8.

———. 1971. 'Wendy and Wazza Caught in the Act'. 24 April, 5.

Guilliatt, R. 2012. 'That Blockhead Thing'. *The Monthly*, April. collapseboard.com/reviews/live-reviews/wendy-saddington-and-peter-head-camelot-lounge-marrickville-sydney-29-04-12/ (accessed 10 February 2015).

Juddery, M. 2006. 'Almost Famous'. *Weekend Australian*, 18–19 February, 6.

Kent, D. M. 1998 (unpublished). *Go-Set: Life and Death of an Australian Pop Magazine*, milesago.com/press/go-set.htm (accessed 10 February 2015).

Leatherdale, J. 2014. 'Still Switched On: Illuminating the Many Facets of Light Artist Roger Folly-Fogg'. *Oz Arts*. ozarts.net.au/images/ozarts/2014-autumn/ROGER%20FOLEY%20for%20web.pdf (accessed 10 February 2016).

Levin, D. 2013. 'RIP Chrissy Amphlett 1969–2013'. *Fasterlouder*, 22 April. fasterlouder.junkee.com/rip-chrissy-amphlett-1959-2013/832988 (accessed 10 February 2015).

Lindy. 1969. 'Wendy Only Wants to be in it up to her Waist'. *Go-Set*, 7 June, 3.

MacLean, S. 1971a. 'Wendy's Done It'. *Go-Set*, 5 June, 14.

———. 1971b. 'Wendy Back with Copperwine'. *Go-Set*, 20 November, 2.

———. 1972. 'Wendy's New Face'. *Go-Set*, 20 May, 18.

Maloney, Peter. 2015. Personal communication with author, 2 October.

———. 2016. Floor talk, 'Wendy Saddington: Underground Icon exhibition', Canberra Museum and Gallery, 3 February.

Marks, I. D. 2006. 'The Year in Australian Rock Music'. In *Tomorrow is Today: Australia in the Psychedelic Era, 1966–1970*, edited by I. McIntyre, 130–143. Adelaide: Wakefield Press.

McFarlane, I. 1999. 'Wendy Saddington'. In *The Encyclopedia of Australian Rock and Roll*, 543–544. Sydney: Allen & Unwin.

———. 2011. 'Wendy Saddington & the Copperwine Live'. CD Liner Notes.

———. 2013. 'Vale Wendy Saddington'. *Addicted to Noise*, 15 July. addictedtonoise.com.au/vale-wendy-saddington/ (accessed 10 February 2015).

McIntyre, I. 2006a. 'Go-Set 1966'. In *Tomorrow is Today: Australia in the Psychedelic Era, 1966–1970*, edited by I. McIntyre, 23–32. Adelaide: Wakefield Press.

———. 2006b. 'Wendy Saddington'. In *Tomorrow is Today: Australia in the Psychedelic Era, 1966–1970*, edited by I. McIntyre, 186–193. Adelaide: Wakefield Press.

Meldrum, I. 1968. 'Caught in the Act'. *Go-Set*, 17 July, 9.

Moore, C. 1994. *Indecent Exposures: Twenty Years of Australian Feminist Photography*. Sydney: Allen & Unwin.

Nelligan, K. 2016. 'Lady Gaga vs Lorde: Why Both Tributes Captured the Essence of David Bowie'. *The Conversation*, 2 March. theconversation.com/lady-gaga-vs-lorde-why-both-tributes-captured-the-essence-of-david-bowie-55507 (accessed 10 March 2016).

Nimmervoll, E. 1971. 'Wendy Wants to Split'. *Go-Set*, 14 August, 10.

Nugent, D. 1972. 'Wendy Saddington and Copperwine Live'. *Go-Set*, 16 September, 16.

——. 1973. 'Wendy Saddington: Sydney'. *Go-Set*, 1 December, 20.

Raffaele, G. 1969. 'An Exciting Swinger'. *The Canberra Times*, 15 March, 15.

Riley, E. 2016. 'What the Debate Around Triple J's Hottest 100 Misses About Privilege'. *The Guardian*, 27 January. theguardian.com/music/2016/jan/27/what-the-debate-around-triple-js-hottest-100-misses-about-privilege (accessed 28 January 2016).

Saddington, W. 1970. 'Not Just a Dream'. *Go-Set*, 4 February.

Samantha. 1969. 'She's Sweet with an Edge of Bitterness'. *Go-Set*, 6 September, 23.

Schwartz, L. 2012. 'Blue Moon Rising for Saddington'. *Sydney Morning Herald*, 10 December. smh.com.au/entertainment/music/blue-moon-rising-for-saddington-20121209-2b41j.html (accessed 2 October 2015).

St John, J. 2013. 'Wendy's Eulogy' [on file with author].

Stewart, K. 2006. 'Perfumed Farts'. *Meanjin* 65 (3): 132–137.

Stoves, R. 1971. 'Wendy Saddington'. *Daily Planet,* 24 November, 6.

Stratton, J. 2008. 'A Jew Singing Like a Black Woman in Australia: Race, Renée Geyer and Marcia Hines'. *Journal of Popular Music Studies* 20 (2): 166–193. doi.org/10.1111/j.1533-1598.2008.00155.x

Strong, C. 2010. 'The Triple J Hottest 100 of All Time and Dominance of the Rock Canon'. *Meanjin* 69 (2): 122–127.

———. 2015. 'All the Girls in Town: The Missing Women of Australian Rock, Cultural Memory and Coverage of the Death of Chrissy Amphlett'. *Perfect Beat* 15 (2): 149–166. doi.org/10.1558/prbt.v15i2.18363

———. 2016. 'How Will "Molly" Help us Remember Australian Culture?'. *The Conversation*, 5 February. theconversation.com/how-will-molly-help-us-remember-australian-culture-54117 (accessed 5 February 2016).

True, E. 2015. 'Looking Through a Window by Wendy Saddington—Australia's First Lady of Soul'. *The Guardian*, 24 February. theguardian.com/music/2015/feb/24/looking-through-a-window-by-wendy-saddington-australias-first-lady-of-soul (accessed 2 October 2015).

Vogt, R. 2005. 'Thump'n Pig & Puff'n Billy—Downunda'. *Faster-Louder*, 19 September. fasterlouder.junkee.com/thumpn-pig-puffn-billy-downunda/774866 (accessed 12 March 2016).

Watts, R. 2013. 'Vale Wendy Saddington'. *ArtsHub*, June 25. artshub.com.au/news-article/news/performing-arts/vale-wendy-saddington-195791 (accessed 2 October 2015).

Whiteley, S. 2013. 'Popular Music, Gender and Sexualities'. *IASPM@Journal* 3 (2): 78–85. doi.org/10.5429/2079-3871(2013)v3i2.6en

Discography

'Looking Through a Window'/'We Need a Song'. 1971. Infinity Records Australia.

Soulful Sisters: From the 60s and 70s. 2013. Sony Music Australia.

Then & Now: Australia Salutes The Beatles. 2014. Abacus edition, Universal Music Australia.

Wendy Saddington & The Copperwine Live. 1971. Infinity Records Australia.

Wendy Saddington & The Copperwine Live. 2011. Aztec Records Australia.

Wendy Saddington Looking Through a Window. 1972. Infinity Records Australia.

Audiovisual References

3 Directions in Australian Pop Music. 1972. Commonwealth Film Unit.

Fusions. 1969. ABC Production.

Long Way to the Top. 2001. ABC Music Production.

Once Around the Sun. 2012. David Hugget and Gordon Mutch, Umbrella.

RocKwiz. 2012. Episode 133, 12 November. SBS Australian Production.

Wendy Saddington and Friends. 1972. ABC Production.

Social Media

Go-Set 50th Anniversary. 2016. *Sydney Morning Herald.* smh.com.au/interactive/2016/school-of-pop/ (accessed 10 October 2016).

Wendy Saddington Facebook page. facebook.com/Wendy-Saddington-348099395218233/timeline (accessed 10 October 2016).

6

Unsung Heroes: Recreating the Ensemble Dynamic of Motown's Funk Brothers

Vincent Perry

Introduction

By the early 1960s, the genre known as soul had become the most commercially successful of all the crossover styles. Drawing on musical influences from the genres of gospel, jazz and blues, 'soul's success was as much due to a number of labels, so-called "house sounds", and little-known bands, as it was to specific performers or songwriters' (Borthwick and Moy, 2004, p. 5). Following on from the pioneer releases of Ray Charles and Sam Cooke, a Detroit-based independent label would soon become the 'most successful and high profile of all the soul labels' (Borthwick and Moy, 2004, p. 5).

Throughout the early 1960s, Berry Gordy's Tamla Motown dominated the domestic US pop and R&B charts with its assembly-line approach to music production (Moorefield, 2005, p. 21), which resulted in a distinctive sound that was shared by all the label's artists. However, in 1963, the company 'achieved its international breakthrough' shortly after signing a landmark distribution deal with EMI in the UK (Borthwick and Moy, 2004, p. 5). Gordy's headquarters—a seemingly humble, suburban residence—was ambitiously named Hitsville USA and, throughout the 1960s, it became a hub for pop record success. Emerson (2005, p. 194) acknowledged Motown's industry presence when he noted:

> Motown was muscling in on the market for dance music. Streamlined, turbo-charged singles by the Marvelettes, Martha and the Vandellas, and the Supremes rolled off the Detroit assembly line ... Berry Gordy's 'Sound of Young America' challenged the Brill Building, 1650 Broadway, and 711 Fifth Avenue as severely as the British Invasion because it proved that black artists did not need white writers to reach a broad pop audience.

Using a model established by Jerome 'Jerry' Leiber and Mike Stoller a few years earlier, Gordy entrusted both songwriting and production duties to a collection of specialised individuals and teams to create new recorded material. Further, this African-American entrepreneur saw the immense 'commercial potential in producing records that could cross over from the rhythm-and-blues charts onto the pop charts' (Covach and Flory, 2012, p. 224), Gordy decided to produce and market his recordings to be 'acceptable to white listeners in their original versions', thus preventing covers of his songs by white artists—a strategy adopted from Chuck Berry (Covach and Flory, 2012, p. 224).

However, much of the stardom and financial return were shared by only a select few involved in the production processes. While the singers became household names and the songwriters prospered with royalty earnings, recording session instrumentalists remained largely unacknowledged. The collection of musicians in question was the Motown house band known as the Funk Brothers. Gordy recruited many of these men after they were discovered performing in various Detroit jazz lounges and clubs. From their basement recording space— affectionately called the Snake Pit—they were hired to record the rhythm section beds[1] for songs that would soon take the US and the world by storm. According to scholarly literature, the Funk Brothers were central to Motown's early success. Lozito (2001, p. 86), pays homage to this house band and his respect for these instrumentalists is clear when he stated:

---

1   The Motown rhythm section beds would often consist of a drummer (sometimes two drummers on separate drum sets), electric/upright bassist, three electric guitarists, multiple keyboardists, a tambourine player and a mallet percussionist (predominantly vibraphone) (Justman, 2002). The collective task of the rhythm sections of this era was to establish a solid foundation for the singers, instrumental soloists and other members of the ensemble that focused on the melody (Covach and Flory, 2012, p. 17).

There were many elements and individuals who combined to make Motown great, and there were none more so than the backing musicians. Together they were the rock on which the empire was built.

Their technical proficiency as session musicians became well known in recording circles. Covach and Flory (2012, p. 125) noted, 'these players were adept at creating their parts on the spot, often without the benefit of scored-out parts or even a completed formal design'. Based on the existing literature that investigates the operations and business ethics of Motown, it is evident that Gordy certainly 'knew the worth of his Detroit musicians' (George, 2003). However:

> That didn't mean he paid them top dollar until he had to, and it didn't mean he felt they should be stars. None of Motown's albums carried the musicians' credits until the seventies. The musicians were never cited by name in interviews with artists, producers, or executives during the sixties. (p. 119)

As a popular music scholar, I was also relatively unaware of the contributions of the Funk Brothers. Further, I have often wondered, 'What exact factors contributed to the Motown backing band's success?'. Was it simply just musicianship and camaraderie among the ensemble that influenced Motown's iconic records? Did the audio engineering limitations[2] of 1960s recording technology demand and promote better time efficiency and musical performances? Did the small confines of Motown's basement recording room provide the band with the ideal environment to record as an ensemble? And, lastly, why weren't these instrumentalists properly credited for their musical contributions?

To answer these questions, I proposed a recording/research project to investigate the Funk Brother's formula for success. As a music practitioner and academic, I proposed an ethnographic and practice-led research project. I assembled a collection of Brisbane-based musicians (informally referred to as the Brisbane Jam Fam) and asked them to collaborate with me to compose, record, arrange and produce a new album called *Soul Sundays*, which would consist of 10 Motown-inspired tracks. It is important to note that most Motown songwriters did not perform as instrumentalists on their respective tracks. This specific practice-led

---

2   The audio engineering limitations of the 1960s are in comparison to the recording technology of today. Further, the recording technology utilised at Motown during the 1960s would have been considered cutting edge at the time.

project is inspired by the work of Smokey Robinson, Stevie Wonder[3] and Marvin Gaye—three individuals known for composing, producing and performing on their own releases.

Our goal with this album was to take on the role of a Funk Brothers–inspired backing band and embrace some 1960s recording practices within the context of a new record production. This chapter is largely based on reflections of the recording of the rhythm section beds for *Soul Sundays*. My reflections are taken from various points of view to best investigate the Motown rhythm section. Throughout this chapter, I will refer to my research questions and aims from the perspective of the instrumentalist, the singer/songwriter and the producer.

The Funk Brothers and Influential Members

The Motown instrumentalists central to this research share origins with numerous African-Americans. Throughout the first half of the twentieth century, many of the Funk Brothers and their respective families migrated north from various Southern states to find employment and escape the segregation that affected every aspect of their daily lives. Lured by the thriving automotive industry and a chance for a better way of life, several instrumentalists who would later become regular session musicians at Motown found work on the assembly lines of Detroit's car factories. Nevertheless, musical ambition and stardom drove these individuals to chase after something more prestigious and profitable. Berry Gordy and his recording label provided them an alternative career path and opportunity to leave the car industry for good. However, the payment for a recording session at Hitsville USA was not a substantial increase to their previous factory wages. Between 1959 and 1960, it is documented that the Funk Brothers received a payment of US$5 and a bowl of soup per session.[4] Further, these recording artists were almost never acknowledged in the liner notes of record releases and were sternly prohibited from recording on their own or with any Motown rivals.[5]

---

3   By the 1970s, 'Wonder played most of the instruments on his albums, overdubbing drums, guitar, bass and keyboards' (DeCurtis, Henke and George-Warren, 1992, p. 298).
4   'Berry [Gordy] was gradually able to raise the pay scale of his studio musicians from the initial $5 a side to $7.25, $10, $15, and eventually several years later, the union scale of $52.50 a session' (Slutsky, Jamerson and Gordy, 1989, p. 13).
5   It is important to note that this was common among other labels such as Chess and Sun Records.

Hitsville USA was home to numerous session instrumentalists. However, Earl Van Dyke, William 'Benny' Benjamin and James Jamerson 'were the key men … They were Motown's backbone, the men who played the music that made America dance' (George, 2003, p. 119). Aside from his performances on piano and organ, Van Dyke's roles as bandleader and 'studio organiser' (Lozito, 2001, p. 87) were equally essential to the productivity and direction of each recording session.

Regarding Benjamin's contribution, Slutsky (1998, p. 41) noted:

> You need to hear only the intro to Martha & the Vandellas' 'Dancing in the Street' to know where Benny Benjamin was coming from: energy and attitude. He also excelled at subtle kickdrum shadings, deft brush work, and the originality of his beats.

Slutsky also acknowledges Benjamin as the creator of the 'Motown drum beat': a rhythmic measure that features a constant quarter-note snare-drum pattern. This beat is regularly heard on Stevie Wonder's 'Uptight' (1965) and during the chorus section of The Temptations' 'Get Ready' (1965). Even though the bass drum pattern varies, the hi-hat and snare-drum patterns largely remain the same throughout the duration of these mentioned tracks. Benjamin's drumbeat quickly became a recurring theme in many other hit records and was adopted by all Motown drummers. From a drumming standpoint, I believe this drumbeat became an authentic rhythmic feature that allowed Motown to remain relatively distinctive among other soul labels. Tragically, Benjamin's personal flaw was his alcohol and drug dependence; in 1968, his self-abusive lifestyle led to his untimely death. Despite the passing of this influential artist, Motown was fortunate to have two other drummers able to deputise for Benjamin. Regarded by Slutsky as 'the master of the Motown shuffle', Richard 'Pistol' Allen provided drum arrangements on hit records such as The Four Tops' 1965 release 'I Can't Help Myself (Sugar Pie Honey Bunch)'.

The second-most prominent musician who carried on Benjamin's legacy was Uriel Jones—a drummer best known for his driving beat on the Marvin Gaye/Tammi Terrell duet 'Ain't No Mountain High Enough' (1967). During an interview for a magazine article, even Jones acknowledged Benny Benjamin as the most respected of the Motown drummers among the instrumentalists who recorded for this label.

According to Jones:

> Papa Zita [Benjamin's nickname] invented that Motown beat, and he taught it to us. Because of all his problems, we probably played drums on more Motown hits than he did. But he was Funk Brother #1. (Slutsky, 1998, p. 41)

If Benjamin was the number one drummer, then James Jamerson was the most revered Motown bassist amid his peers. In simple terms, he was regarded as 'the player who everybody wanted on their sessions' (Lozito, 2001, p. 87). Respected musician and producer Don Was claims that Jamerson's bass contributions on Motown recordings are 'the height of creativity ... freedom and experimentation and fearlessness' (Justman, 2002). Probably the most remarkable feature of Jamerson's technique was that he performed all his bass parts with only his left hand and right index finger. According to his son, James Jamerson III, 'he played on all those hits with one finger. It was called the "hook"' (Justman, 2002). However, like Benjamin, Jamerson also sadly suffered from alcoholism. 'The ensuing deterioration of Jamerson's physical and mental health caused Motown to bring in Bob Babbitt to fill the void' (Slutsky, 1998, p. 41). His depression only intensified when the Motown recording company decided, without warning, to move its operations and headquarters to Los Angeles. His tragic death in 1983 was directly related to his alcoholism and depression. Despite the tragic endings to these musicians' lives, Benny Benjamin and James Jamerson are still regarded as the quintessential Motown rhythm section; understanding their musical partnership is integral in the creation of a Motown-inspired backing band.

House Bands and Recording in the Shadows

At this point in the article, it is very important to note that the Funk Brothers were certainly not the only prolific house band working in the US recording industry during the 1960s and 1970s. Further, it was common for record labels to not credit specific instrumentalists in the record liner notes. Consequently, their identities were often unknown to the public. It is clear that most US bands of this period rarely experienced any fame. Williams (2010, p. 59) commented:

6. UNSUNG HEROES

Popular music in particular supports a celebrity system centered on highly visible and easily identifiable individuals. Yet much popular music is in fact made by unknown, unidentified musicians, hired collaborators who work out of the public eye in the recording studio or in the shadows of the concert stage.

It is my opinion that today's recording artists should be aware of and celebrate the 'unidentified musicians' of the 1960s and 1970s for their respective recording contributions. They may not be considered stars (compared to lead vocalists) by the public; however, they should be remembered for performing the instrumental contributions that formed the foundation of most popular music tracks of this era. Exactly why the session musicians of this period remained largely uncelebrated and unknown is debatable.

On the west coast of the US, record producer Phil Spector made heavy use of a backing band known as the Wrecking Crew. Throughout the 1960s and early 1970s, this prolific backing band provided the rhythm section beds on hit records by The Beach Boys, Frank Sinatra, Nancy Sinatra, Sonny and Cher, Elvis, The Monkees and many more artists. Directed by the son of Wrecking Crew guitarist Tommy Tedesco, the 2014 documentary *The Wrecking Crew* provides an insight into the Los Angeles recording industry of the 1960s and 1970s, as well as interviews with many famous recording artists who had recorded with this relatively unidentified backing band. In the film, Brian Wilson describes this band as 'the focal point of the music' and the individuals 'with all the spirit and all the know-how especially for rock and roll music' (Tedesco, 2014). Nancy Sinatra also displays her admiration when she labels these instrumentalists as 'the unsung heroes of all those hit records'. However, there is also a general feeling of frustration conveyed by some of the film's interviewees, and this is evident later in the documentary when Mickey Dolenz (of The Monkees) notes:

> The producers made a big mistake when they didn't put the credits on the back of their albums of all the people who had played on the albums. Not only did they deserve it, but I think it was misleading.

The conclusion I can draw from this documentary is that the Wrecking Crew—like their Detroit-based counterparts the Funk Brothers—were highly valued for their musical talents in the recording studio, but heavily underappreciated and unknown by the public.

Thankfully, there is some valuable literature available that explores the role and importance of the session musicians that make up these 'house bands'. Zak III's *The Poetics of Rock: Cutting Tracks, Making Records* (2001) provides a scholar's perspective on the collaborative process of recording production. Zak III reflects:

> Making records is intrinsically a collaborative creative process, involving the efforts of a 'composition team' whose members interact in various ways. As a matter of form, the 'artist' on a recording is usually the person or group who receives top billing on the album cover, but in fact most of the tasks involved in making a record require some measure of artistry. Social relationships among the team members also contribute to the outcome of a recording project. (p. 163)

Although this passage is found in the chapter entitled 'Engineers and Producers', I believe the 'composition team' to which Zak III refers to is a group of creative individuals that also includes session musicians. Campelo (2015) continues the theme of celebrating and highlighting the work of all who contribute to the music production process. As part of her concluding thoughts, this professional musician and scholar passionately proclaims:

> It is my firm belief that session musicians should earn more credit for their anonymous work, on a general as well as an academic level. It would be important to clarify the type of contribution that these truly 'hidden musicians', using Ruth Finnegan's expression (Finnegan, 1989), gave to music cultures associated to popular music. (p. 7)

I agree with Campelo's comments regarding session musicians. Further, I believe all present and future music productions should accurately and honestly list all musical contributions in liner notes on each record. Irrespective of the payment for a performance, every individual who contributes to a popular music production—or any recording production for that matter—deserves to be credited for his or her respective involvement.

Research Aims and Questions

Following the work of Zak III and Campelo, this practice-led research project aims to highlight the contributions of 'hidden musicians'. In addition, a major goal of this project and research paper was to situate my proposed rhythm section in the 'shoes' of the Funk Brothers.

As a 'compositional team', we wanted to investigate the mental, physical, emotional and musical pressures these session musicians endured during the production of Motown records. Time is one the most precious commodities in a recording session and it is my belief that the recording label in question was an expert in maximising its creative time. According to Motown's vibraphonist and tambourine player, Jack Ashford:

> They [the Motown producers] would allow for four songs for a three-hour session and we would get no less than two. But that's because the same group of guys played together all the time ... The only thing that changed was the changes. It was a home there. We spent so much time there. (Justman, 2002)

With this information in mind, it was my goal as the producer of *Soul Sundays* to record a minimum of two tracks per session.

Also, a primary ambition was to uncover the elements of Motown's live recording process that are applicable to modern record production. This style of recording is logistically more ambitious than the standard multi-track method that my collaborators and I are used to—this method generally involves recording each instrument separately. With this current recording project, I hoped to embrace the house band concept of recording a rhythm section bed as a full rhythm section.

Another major aim for this research was to create an ideal room for the recording of the live backing band that forms the foundation of the entire production. Throughout my undergraduate years, the topic of 'space' was often discussed in the context of acoustics and ambience.[6] However, the subject of space in relation to the research at hand pertains to the other focus of ensemble unity. I believe the Motown basement recording room heavily influenced the interpersonal interactions between the session musicians. This confined work area may have presented numerous sonic challenges, but from a positive standpoint, it forced the band to work as united recording team. Again, it is important to note that the session musicians at Chess, Sun Records and Atlantic would have worked in similar recording spaces to their Motown counterparts.

For many of my collaborators, the idea of recording in the basement of a house is quite a foreign concept due to their previous experience of working in various commercial studios in South East Queensland.

---

6   See Doyle (2005) for a comprehensive analysis of the ambience used in twentieth century popular music productions.

This choice of location may also be viewed as a budget option compared to recording in an existing, purpose-built facility. However, I intentionally chose the basement setting to better understand how this type of space influences the musical interactions between collaborators. I was particularly interested to explore how a basement studio affected my collaborators' individual performances during the recording sessions.

In preparation for the recording sessions, I aimed to source historically appropriate instruments and recording equipment. It intended to set up a completely analogue recording studio with instruments manufactured and assembled during the 1960s and 1970s. Following the work of Bennett (2012) and Bates (2012), I wanted to examine whether vintage instruments and equipment had any influence on our musical performance in the confines of our studio space.

Sourcing drums for this research was straightforward, as I already owned a collection of 1960s Ludwig drums in different dimensions and sizes. Glen Hunt (guitarist) was kind enough to lend his vintage Fender Precision Bass (the same bass make and model of Motown's James Jamerson and Bob Babbitt) to our bassist, Tim Hatch. A set of flatwound strings was purchased to complement the Fender P-Bass tone to recreate the bass tones of Jamerson.[7] On the subject of keyboard sounds, we sourced a 1959 Hammond B-3 organ (which we amplified through a Leslie Cabinet), a 1970s Wurlitzer Electric Piano, a 1970s Rhodes Electric Piano Mark 1 and a 1967 Kawai upright piano. Finally, we hired a Tascam MS16 reel-to-reel recorder as our recording device. From a historical perspective, this specific device was not historically appropriate due to its assembly in the 1980s. However, this specific model was selected because it was the most vintage multi-track tape machine available for hire. Also, from an audio engineering perspective, a major positive feature of this specific model was that it provided our production with 16 separate threads—we hoped this feature would make the mixing process easier. Overall, this obsession with sourcing vintage gear may be viewed as simply technostalgia.[8] However, I believe that giving my collaborators the appropriate tools would aid our band to recreate the Funk Brothers' dynamic and sounds.

---

7   'An essential element of ' "the Jamerson Sound" [was] heavy gauge Labella flatwound strings' (Slutsky et al., 1989, p. 85).
8   See Williams (2015) and Bennett (2012) for dissections of technostalgia.

Method

Assembling an appropriate backing band for the *Soul Sundays* recording project was fortunately a simple task. First, I approached musicians that participated in my last research/recording project (Perry, 2012) and the subsequent Motown tribute show: Vincent Perry's Motown Revue. Three of my collaborators (Kevin Suierveld, Tim Hatch and Travis Lee) were my classmates during my undergraduate years and we had almost a decade of experience working together on various musical projects (see Table 6.1). Excepting Phil Mairu, every musician in my proposed personnel list was a current colleague of mine in one of the various function/corporate bands in South East Queensland. All members of the band regularly attended local jam nights and music social events as part of a group of musicians informally known as the Brisbane Jam Fam. We are all fans of Motown records and share a similar music vocabulary/repertoire.

Table 6.1: Years of mutual experience with my collaborators

Artist name	Instrument/s	Years of mutual experience with me
Kevin Suierveld	Congas	Nine
Tim Hatch	Bass	Nine
Travis Lee	Vocals	Ten
Mitch Pattugalan	Piano and keyboards	Six
Dan Wolsner	Piano and keyboards	Two
Glen Hunt	Electric guitar	Three
Xell Newton	Vocals	Three
Brett Orr	Keyboards	Three
Phil Mairu	Tambourine	None

Before we could arrange, record and produce an album of new tracks, our first job as an ensemble was to write new repertoire. Several members of the proposed backing band are respected singer/songwriter/producers in their own right. This meant that multiple members of the band acted as both songwriters and instrumentalists during the production of the album. Conveniently, Dan Wolsner and Brett Orr had previously written both the tracks that they were contributing to the album prior to the project—these four tracks were stylistically appropriate for the research. Travis Lee, Kevin Suierveld, Mitch Pattugalan and Xell Newton (collaborating with Tim Hatch, Glen Hunt and Chris Sheehy) all wrote new material specifically for the album (see Table 6.2). Between May 2014 and April 2015, I organised arranging/jam sessions on various Sundays to work on the material. Sunday was the only day of the week when we could regularly meet and collaborate. This almost-weekly ritual became the inspiration for the album title: *Soul Sundays*.[9]

Table 6.2: Track listing, songwriting credits and record date details for *Soul Sundays*

#	Song title	Songwriter/s	Vocalist	Record date
1	'We'll Get Together'	Dan Wolsner	Dan Wolsner	15/05/15
2	'Just You and I'	Travis Lee and Kevin Suierveld	Travis Lee	16/05/15
3	'Masterpiece'	Mitch Pattugalan	Mitch Pattugalan	22/05/15
4	'Real Love'	Mitch Pattugalan	Mitch Pattugalan	22/05/15
5	'The Least That You Can Do (Smile)'	Brett Orr	Brett Orr	23/05/15
6	'Chemistry'	Brett Orr	Brett Orr	24/05/15
7	'Now You're Gone (So Very Happy)'	Xell Newton and Glen Hunt	Xell Newton	29/05/15
8	'Second Opinion'	Xell Newton, Chris Sheehy and Tim Hatch	Xell Newton	29/05/15
9	'Change'	Dan Wolsner	Dan Wolsner	30/05/15
10	'Always'	Travis Lee and Kevin Suierveld	Travis Lee	30/05/15

During the arranging and preproduction process, we carefully listened to and analysed iconic Motown records (on vinyl when possible) for directions on instrumentation, songwriting elements and audio production components. *The Supremes A' Go-Go* (1966), *The Motown Story (Volume One)* (1971), *What's Going On* (1971) and Stevie Wonder's *Songs in the Key of Life* (1976) became essential listening as I acquired each album on LP. To properly analyse the sonic texture of these records, I made a conscious decision to avoid listening to any MP3 or remastered versions of these Motown releases. Further, when possible, we tried to source vintage instruments to replicate sounds and textures heard on Motown releases.

---

9   See Thompson and Lashua (2014) for other studio-based ethnographic research.

Figure 6.1: Our backing band recording in the temporary basement recording studio: (from left to right) Dan Wolsner, Mitch Pattugalan, Vincent Perry, Tim Hatch, Glen Hunt and Kevin Suierveld
Source: Perry (2012).

Next, we installed a temporary recording space/studio in the basement of a suburban house. Band members Tim Hatch and Xell Newton were kind enough to volunteer their home in Salisbury for the preproduction process (writing and arranging) and their subsequent house in Mansfield[10] for the recording of rhythm section beds. As discussed in the section covering the research questions, we had previous experience recording together in a large-format recording studio.[11] After that album production, I understood that a large recording room with tall ceilings was not ideal when trying to replicate the Motown sound. Further, it was my theory that if we could record in a basement, we might be able to replicate the sonic characteristics of Motown's recording room.

Between 15 and 30 May 2015, we recorded all the rhythm section beds for the 10 proposed tracks. When possible, we tracked each song with the entire rhythm section present. Colleague and former classmate James Fox Higgins was hired as audio engineer. During the recording sessions, he was in the control booth in the adjoining room. His main role on the first day of recording was to help set up microphones in appropriate locations,

---

10   Salisbury and Mansfield are suburbs of Brisbane.
11   Studio A and room 1 at the Queensland Conservatorium's Gold Coast campus (Griffith University) were used during the previous research project (Perry, 2012).

assign channel volume levels via an analogue console and operate the 16-channel tape machine he had hired to our band for the project. After the first day of recording, everything was left in place for the following two weeks so we could simply return to the studio, turn on the appropriate equipment and carry on where we had left off.

I purchased a 1-in reel of analogue tape to record in conjunction with James's Tascam MS16 reel-to-reel recorder. We limited our number of takes for each song based on the duration of the reel. In most cases, we achieved a maximum of eight takes on each reel (for the shorter songs). After we recorded a take that all rhythm section instrumentalists were satisfied with, we recorded/transferred all passes of each song to Pro Tools 10 (my preferred digital audio workstation) via two 8-channel Focusrite Sapphire Pro40 interfaces. I chose to transfer these recordings to Pro Tools, as we only had access to the reel-to-reel recorder during these first three weekends of the production. Further, I planned to record a series of overdubs (vocals, strings, brass and percussion tracks) over the coming months in various different recording studios. My laptop and Pro Tools software allowed me to easily edit, comp[12] and transfer audio data without the usage and transportation of a reel-to-reel recorder.

As there was only one tape reel, we erased the tape after each track to record the next song. This recording limitation promoted a sense of finalisation after each track and clearly motivated a higher level of musical performance among my collaborators. As part of documenting the creative process and work environment, I hired filmmaker Mason Hoffman and his assistants to film all recording sessions. The video footage captured was very valuable when I began to reflect on the rhythm section recording process.

Results, Outcomes and Reflections

Recording one song can be a very time-consuming process. Originally, I booked in the band and hired the recording gear for two weekends (four sessions in total) with the goal of recording the 10 proposed tracks. In hindsight, this was not nearly enough time. It ended up taking seven separate sessions over three weeks to record all the rhythm section beds. Also, I did not allocate sufficient time to set up the immense amount of recording and musical gear in our basement studio. Further, we were only

---

12 See Senior (2011) for a definition and explanation of the process of audio comping.

able to track one song on the first day because I underestimated the time taken to sound check microphone levels and ensure everyone had quality headphone monitoring. My poor time management heavily affected my creativity and drumming performance. On more than one occasion, I was more concerned with keeping up with my unrealistic recording schedule than worrying about the quality of the actual tracks. This time pressure also affected my individual mood, which affected my fellow recording artists and their respective performances. On a positive note, productivity did improve over the three weekends because we naturally became more comfortable in the surroundings of the basement studio. Our ensemble dynamic noticeably improved during this challenging process and each completed track developed our confidence as a band.

Tracking live as a band is challenging for all those involved. This specific process requires a group of multiple musicians to record together—often in a single space—to achieve a collective goal. It is frequently stressful, tiring and occasionally intimidating being in the presence of peers. Also, there is a small margin of error when recording whole rhythm section beds. Each musician relies on each other to execute his or her respective parts and the pressure of not disappointing your fellow band mates can often create a deep sense of anxiety and internal pressure. However, when our band was able to record a full take, it felt like a genuine achievement and a true team effort. When we played back each take, we could hear how individual performances were combined to create a unified music recording; personal anxiety and stress were now replaced with collective relief and euphoria.

It occurred to me on the second day of the recording project that the anxiety regarding my individual performance should be replaced with encouraging thoughts and positive energy. Instead of worrying about making mistakes, I was motivated to inspire the musicians around me by performing to the best of my ability and laying down a solid drum part on every take. Further, I eventually discovered that my positive energy and presence were more valuable than a solid drum performance. The simple act of smiling and demonstrating that I was enjoying the experience (of working with the group) benefited those around me in the room. We were much more efficient as an ensemble when we were having fun and our respective body language influenced the collective mood in the room. Brett Orr reflected on the recording process and noted, 'When you're looking up at Tim [band bassist] and he's just grinning his arse off, as opposed to someone who is just staring at a chart—it's a big difference' (personal communication, 16 January 2016). Brett's reflection reminded me of the importance of sharing positive emotion with your fellow instrumentalists. I believe that Tim's simple act of smiling improved the collective mood of the studio and it acknowledged that he was enjoying sharing that moment working as an ensemble.

The other major benefit of recording as an ensemble was that we were forced to listen to each other's parts in relation to our own individual part. I believe that the chordal players—Glen (electric guitar), Mitch (keyboards) and Dan (keyboards)—benefited from recording together because they often wrote and arranged their respective parts at the same time during each take. This trial-and-error style of arranging would occasionally result in one or more musicians spoiling a quality take. However, if a musical idea (such as a keyboard lick or riff) was too complicated, dissonant or unfitting for the song, we instantly knew based on body language and hearing each other. Conceptually, recording each song was similar to a group of people assembling a jigsaw puzzle together.

Further, there were feelings of finalisation after each take because we knew we were recording to tape as a band. It was quite liberating to commit to a part and not be concerned about performance errors that needed to be repaired in the post-production phase. This style of recording promoted better ownership of our performance—both individually and collectively as an ensemble. Also, by tracking together, we saved the time normally allocated to tracking each instrument individually. Instead of organising a full day to record guitar or piano parts, we dedicated time to recording a complete rhythm section bed.

The experiment of working in a temporary basement recording studio/room provided an encouraging and welcoming space for creative work and it 'didn't feel like there was any financial/time pressure' during the sessions (Brett Orr, personal communication, 16 January 2016). Financially, this project was a fairly affordable venture. Conversely, large-format recording studios are expensive to hire and don't always provide a space in which musicians can feel comfortable or creative. Considering the decline of profits in the recording industry over the past 15 years,[13] this method of home recording presents a sustainable and affordable option for producers (such as myself) to efficiently record full ensembles on a regular basis.

---

13 'Over the past 15 years, there has been a decline in large corporate owned studios and a rise in smaller independently owned, producer-based studios. Many of these studios are in private homes, owned by a mixture of hobbyists and professionals. Here, producers own and operate their own studio, often functioning as both a sound engineer and musician' (O'Grady, 2014, p. 103).

Concluding Thoughts

It is difficult to comprehend the pressures and challenges experienced by the Funk Brothers (or other notable house bands) throughout the 1960s and 1970s. However, after forming a backing band modelled on the Funk Brothers and recording an album of Motown-inspired original songs, I have a greater understanding of the interpersonal skills required to be an efficient rhythm section. Also, this practice-led research demonstrated the level of musicianship required to record rhythm section beds as a full ensemble—something that I had only read about in scholarly work and viewed in documentaries.

Further, recording songs as a complete rhythm section is often a stressful process and allows for a very small margin of error. However, when successfully conducted, this recording method can produce tracks that promote ensemble unity. Also, I believe that the individual instrumentalists involved will mature as recording artists and hone various skills that are valuable to session musicians. During the production of *Soul Sundays*, I observed how my fellow musicians have become more time efficient and technically proficient on his or her respective instruments. This is partly due to the nature of recording together as a section and not individually. While performing my responsibilities as band drummer and musical director, I have witnessed an improvement in my own skills—most notably in my ability to communicate with my peers. I have developed a greater appreciation of both verbal and non-verbal communication in the recording studio. Also, this research has highlighted the importance of band diplomacy. Working in an ensemble requires a group of instrumentalists to respect and trust one another to achieve collective success.

Regarding house bands, the recording community and industry need to applaud and properly credit the contributions of these hidden musicians. The public may only idolise and glorify the performances of vocalists who are the face of a track; however, everyone involved in the compositional team deserves to be celebrated and, at the very least, listed on the liner notes of a record. Stardom may be anointed to a select few; nevertheless, all those who have contributed to a recording should share credit.

The most positive outcome from this research project was the completion of 10 rhythm section beds—the foundation and backbone of 10 original Motown-inspired tracks. Also, each keyboardist who appeared on the album had the opportunity to appear as a lead vocalist on his or her respective tracks. With the release of this album in mid-2017, I am fully aware that there is no guarantee of commercial success and stardom for any of the singer/songwriters. However, this collaborative recording process and study of backing bands of the past has taught me to value and recognise every individual who contributed to the completion of *Soul Sundays*. Finally, it is my hope that many of the revelations and findings of this production will aid me in my future recording projects and research.

References

Bates, E. 2012. 'What Studios Do'. *Journal on the Art of Record Production* 7.

Bennett, S. 2012. 'Endless Analogue: Situating Vintage Technologies in the Contemporary Recording & Production Workplace'. *Journal on the Art of Record Production* 7: 1–18.

Borthwick, S. and R. Moy. 2004. *Popular Music Genres*. Edinburgh: Edinburgh University Press Ltd.

Campelo, I. 2015. 'That Extra Thing—The Role of Session Musicians in the Recording Industry'. *Journal on the Art of Record Production* 10.

Covach, J. and A. Flory. 2012. *What's That Sound?: An Introduction to Rock and its History* (3rd ed.). New York: Norton.

DeCurtis, A., J. Henke and H. George-Warren. 1992. 'Stevie Wonder'. In *The Rolling Stone Illustrated History of Rock & Roll*, edited by J. Miller. London: Plexus Publishing Ltd.

Doyle, P. 2005. *Echo and Reverb: Fabricating Space in Popular Music Recording, 1900–1960*. Middletown: Wesleyan University Press.

Emerson, K. 2005. *Always Magic in the Air: The Bomp and Brilliance of the Brill Building Era*. New York: Viking.

Finnegan, R. 1989. *The Hidden Musicians: Music-Making in an English Town*. Cambridge: Cambridge University Press.

George, N. 2003. *Where Did Our Love Go? The Rise & Fall of the Motown Sound*. London: Omnibus Press (A Division of Music Sales Limited).

Justman, P. (Director). 2002. *Standing in the Shadows of Motown*. Santa Monica, California: Artisan Entertainment.

Lozito, C. 2001. 'Sons of the Snakepit'. In *Calling Out Around the World: A Motown Reader*, edited by K. Abbot. London: Helter Skelter Publishing.

Moorefield, V. 2005. *The Producer as Composer: Shaping the Sounds of Popular Music*. Cambridge: MIT Press.

O'Grady, P. 2014. 'Studio Hubs: Changing Recording Environments'. In *Communities, Places, Ecologies: Proceedings of the 2013 IASPM–ANZ Conference*, edited by J. O'Regan and T. Wren, 103–11. Brisbane: International Association for the Study of Popular Music, Australia and New Zealand Branch.

Perry, V. 2012. *In Search of Soul and Groove: A Study of the Motown Drum Sound*. Queensland Conservatorium, Griffith University.

Senior, M. 2011. 'Comping: Reaper Tips & Techniques'. soundonsound.com/techniques/comping (accessed 20 October 2016).

Slutsky, A. 1998. 'United We Stand: James Jamerson and Benny Benjamin'. *Bass Player* 9: 40–41.

Slutsky, A., J. Jamerson and B. Gordy. 1989. *Standing in the Shadows of Motown: The Life and Music of Legendary Bassist James Jamerson*. Wynnewood: Hal Leonard.

Tedesco, D. (Director). 2014. *The Wrecking Crew*. C. Hope, J. Leonoudakis, M. Linden, C. Scanlon, D. Tedesco and S. G. Tedesco (Producers): Madman Entertainment Pty Ltd.

Thompson, P. and B. Lashua. 2014. 'Getting it on Record: Issues and Strategies for Ethnographic Practice in Recording Studios'. *Journal of Contemporary Ethnography* 43 (3): 746–769. doi.org/10.1177/0891241614530158

Williams, A. 2010. 'Navigating Proximities: The Creative Identity of the Hired Musician'. *Journal of the Music & Entertainment Industry Educators Association* 10 (1): 59–76.

———. 2015. 'Technostalgia and the Cry of the Lonely Recordist'. *Journal on the Art of Record Production* 9.

Zak III, A. J. 2001. *The Poetics of Rock: Cutting Tracks, Making Records*. London: University of California Press. doi.org/10.1525/california/9780520218093.001.0001

Discography

Ashford, N. and V. Simpson. 1967. 'Ain't No Mountain High Enough'. Tamla Motown.

Gaye, M. 1971. *What's Going On*. Motown Record Corporation.

Gordy, B. 1971. *The Motown Story: Volume One*. Motown Record Corporation.

Holland, B., L. Dozier and E. Holland. 1966. *The Supremes A' Go-Go*. Tamla Motown.

Robinson, S. 1965. 'Get Ready'. *Gettin' Ready*. Tamla Motown.

Wonder, S. 1976. *Songs in the Key of Life*. Motown Record Corporation.

Wonder, S., S. Moy and H. Cosby. 1965. 'Uptight (Everything's Alright)'. Tamla Motown.

7

When Divas and Rock Stars Collide: Interpreting Freddie Mercury and Montserrat Caballé's *Barcelona*

Eve Klein

> Mamma mia, what's this? Freddie Mercury, the man who perpetrated heavy-metal opera in 'Bohemian Rhapsody,' shrieking alongside an actual opera star? In 1987 Mercury somehow conned a world-class diva, Montserrat Caballé, to slum with him for an entire album. The result apparently was deemed too flaky to be released in the U.S., but in the wake of Queen's commercial resurgence (and Mercury's death last November from AIDS), any curio is up for grabs. (Farber 1992)

Introduction

This chapter considers Freddie Mercury and Montserrat Caballé's operatic-rock album *Barcelona* (1988) as a logical extension of Mercury's fascination with operatic musical devices, narrative structures and iconography. With this album, two global superstars from divergent musical genres met and brought their musical perspectives into genuine collaboration. However, *Barcelona*, like other popular explorations of opera, has remained largely unexamined because it sits somewhat uncomfortably across art and popular music, agitating anxieties and authenticities as they operate in both terrains.

This chapter will investigate how such anxieties became established by unpacking the circulation of opera within popular recording cultures as elite reproductions of operatic repertory, as 'crossover' music and through its appropriation by popular musicians. This chapter will then conduct an analysis of the *Barcelona* collaboration that situates its creation in the context of Mercury's musical trajectory. Special consideration will be paid to the musical style established in 'Bohemian Rhapsody' (1975). Comparing previous performances to the *Barcelona* album indicates that Mercury and Caballé largely did not attempt to emulate each other's vocal style, but reproduced their existing vocal technique. Despite *Barcelona* exploring musical and vocal terrain already cultivated by Mercury in previous releases, critics had considerable difficulty viewing *Barcelona* as a credible exploration of rock and opera, precisely because Mercury and Caballé occupied the same creative space. Operatic critics aligned Caballé's performance with crossover singing due to the apparent simplicity of the *Barcelona* songs. Rock critics heard Caballé's operatic voice and *Barcelona*'s orchestral accompaniment and viewed it as 'weird' and 'difficult to handle' (Gage, 2012). As the first recording bringing together genuine international stars from their respective genres (see Promane, 2009, p. 140), Mercury and Caballé's collaboration is problematic precisely because it bridged the popular/elite divide from both directions simultaneously.

Contextualisation: Opera within Popular Recording Cultures

This section will unpack the location of opera within twentieth-century popular recording cultures[1] and argue that opera has diverged into three distinct categories on record. The first category is elite reproductions of the operatic canon, usually presented as whole works or concert performances, and whose singers perform primarily in the world's most

---

1 Morton defines recording cultures as encompassing 'the motivations for and the outcomes of the act of recording; the relationships between the creators, promotors, and users of recording technology; and the interactions between people, recording machines, and recordings themselves' (1999, p. 91). The term 'popular recording cultures' is employed in this article to situate recording cultures as occurring within the broader hierarchies of popular culture.

prestigious opera houses. The second category is 'popular' or 'crossover' presentations of operatic repertoire in which singers present selections of popular repertoire, where the material may be arranged or produced to reflect popular music production techniques, and where singers tend to orient their careers around record releases and touring shows. The third category is appropriations of opera into popular music by popular artists who use operatic forms to agitate, critique, add extended narrative coherence, create spectacle or explore more complex approaches to composition within existing genres of popular music. By unpacking the formation of these divisions, we can better understand how *Barcelona* brought different recording cultures into dialogue.

Recording and broadcast technologies such as record players, radios and microphones recast the way Western audiences listened to and engaged with classical music throughout the twentieth century (Morton, 1999, pp. 187–623; Day, 2000, pp. 199–256). The presentation of classical music on recorded media became highly stylised, in part because of the technical limitations and aesthetic practices such media imposed in their early developmental stages (Philip, 2004, pp. 26–62). Excerpts of operas, particularly arias, were popularised on recordings by singers such as Enrico Caruso and Mario Lanza. Despite successful operatic stage careers, both singers became mainstream celebrities whose audiences were most familiar with their voices via records, and, in Lanza's case, also through his film career (Macy, 2009; Hischak, 2009). Macy (2009) notes that Caruso's recordings 'not only made him universally famous; they also did much to encourage the acceptance of recording as a medium for opera … It has been aptly remarked that Caruso made the gramophone and it made him'. Lanza famously played Caruso in the 1951 biopic *The Great Caruso* (Thorpe, 1951).

The relationship between opera and popular music in the twentieth century consists of two interleaved histories. The first history is the evolution of popular opera, or popera, and its persistent tensions with 'serious' music, particularly elite repertory opera. The second is the appropriation of opera, including its styles and motifs, by popular musicians. Day considers that, in the twentieth century, the 'production of recordings required mass markets' and consequently 'music lovers who frequented the opera house and concert hall and played chamber music … at home had never represented more than a small minority of the population at large' (2000, pp. 206–207). Distinctions between repertory opera and popular opera can be charted back to the early twentieth century when classical recordings were promoted to the public as a means of enhancing 'music appreciation', and were considered by figures such as Schoenberg, Adorno and Toye as desensitising audiences and thereby devaluing the experience of music (Day, 2000, pp. 206–210). Importantly, a tradition of sentimental, light-hearted or highly stylised versions of arias continued to be captured even once full-length recordings of entire operas were possible. Adorno (1990) was highly sceptical of early reproduction of opera on short-playing (SP and EP) records in which selections of popular repertoire dominated due to durational restrictions. He was a more optimistic advocate of the longer-form LP record, considering the medium capable of resurrecting the operatic form through its extended temporal dimension (Adorno, 1990, pp. 65–66). However, despite the increased length of recordings made possible by LP records, charismatic and marketable singers like Lanza continued to present arias with contemporary arrangements alongside other popular songs and oriented their careers around singles releases, touring shows and films (see Bessette, 1999). Lanza released over 100 single and EP records from the late 1940s to early 1960s (see Discogs.com, 2016). Despite being one of the most recognised operatic singers of his generation, Lanza's legacy is as an entertainer rather than an opera singer. Arguably, this is at least partially due to Lanza's latter career being focused primarily on recording and broadcast media, rather than in the opera house sanctified by figures such as Adorno. By contrast, Caruso is remembered as an iconic repertory opera singer, because, unlike Lanza, Caruso continued to perform widely in the best-regarded opera houses throughout his recording career (see Macy, 2009). Despite similarities between the two singers and their recording careers, these artists have come to signify the distinction between repertory and popular opera within recording cultures.

The influence of classical vocal style, including smooth register transitions, vibrato, trills and other ornamentation, was evident in popular singing until the early–mid-twentieth century. At this point, popular music vocal production shifted radically towards the vernacular, speech-oriented vocalities of jazz, blues and rock-and-roll, made possible through emerging microphone technologies and necessitated by the co-emergent adoption of instrument amplification and later electrification (see Lockheart, 2003; Potter and Sorrell, 2012, pp. 244–245). Stark (2011, p. 255) considers that crossover singing is a phenomenon in which 'classically trained singers perform in vernacular styles', largely moving from performing classical to popular music. By implication, crossover singers are performing with the assistance of amplification technologies. However, popular opera singers like Lanza, or, later, The Three Tenors, often continued to approach vocal performance using classical vocal techniques (Potter, 1998, p. 187). Therefore, distinction between elite repertory and popular opera can also be made at the level of the recording: by producing records with methods employed in popular music record production; by juxtaposing popular songs with classical repertoire; or by varying the arrangements of canonical arias and songs. Using a variety of devices, popular opera artists have navigated the precarious space between Western art music and Western popular music.

Recording aesthetics have subsequently played out tensions that persist between popular opera and 'serious' classical vocal music. Classical music aficionados compare recordings by contemporary popera singers like Katherine Jenkins, Sarah Brightman, Andrea Bochelli and Il Divo with 'high-brow' reproductions of operatic repertory performed by singers like Renée Fleming, who have distinguished themselves in the world's elite concert halls and opera houses. Musical sales charts like Australia's ARIA charts differentiate releases by labelling them as 'Core Classical' or 'Classical Crossover' (ARIA, 2016). These classifications, made by performing rights organisations and record companies, veil a range of social and cultural preconceptions around the role and value of classical music and the people who consume it. Pejorative distinctions between popular and artistic music, crossover and elite music echo wider anxieties about the threat media cultures have posed to the canonical narratives of Western art practices, including opera (see Morton, 1999, pp. 312–637; Ashby, 2010, p. 8; Klein, 2014).

Popular music possesses a counter-tradition of artists like Freddie Mercury, who have problematised the definitions and distinctions of 'opera' as a musical form through the appropriation of operatic musical devices, narrative structures and iconography into the sphere of popular music. Mercury, the lead singer of UK rock band Queen, was, along with guitarist Brian May, responsible for writing many of the band's international hit releases (Whiteley, 2011). Mercury's eclectic musical taste encompassed a fascination with opera; this interest was thrust upon 1970s rock audiences with the release of 'Bohemian Rhapsody' from the album *A Night at the Opera* (1975). Momentum generated from Queen's rock opera explorations carried through into other music styles. McLeod (2001, p. 194) describes 'Bohemian Rhapsody' as a juxtaposition of hard rock and operatic recitative, aria and chorus forms, utilised to represent a 'world turned upside down, the Bohemia underworld of "Beelzebub" where it is certain that "nothing really matters"'. Further, McLeod argues that 'Bohemian Rhapsody's' underworld motif mimics the 'common tropes in opera, one found in works such as Monteverdi's Orpheo, Purcell's King Arthur, Mozart's Don Giovanni, Weber's Der Freischütz and Wagner's Ring Cycle', with the intent of mocking 'the fascination with moral transgression shared by both opera and rock' (2001, p. 194). McLeod offers a similarly novel analysis of Queen's production techniques by comparing 'the complexity of the 180 choral overdubs' to 'traditional operatic virtuosity and bombast', concluding that the integration of rock and operatic forms is used 'not to lend musical cachet but rather to mock the musical conventions of both opera and rock' (2001, p. 194).

In the wake of 'Bohemian Rhapsody' and the continuation of rock opera and related genres like hip hopera, artists such as Dollie de Luxe, Kate Miller-Heidke and Nina Hagen have continued a tradition of incorporating elements of opera and operatic vocal style into popular releases to add extended narrative coherence, create spectacle and explore more complex approaches to composition within existing genres of popular music. I have written about these appropriations elsewhere in more detail (see Klein, 2013). This music has a different sensibility from popular opera, with singers producing original material or recontextualisations of repertoire that unsettle audience expectations through the signification of opera in rock, pop and related contexts.

'Eccentric' Vocalities? Pairing Mercury with Caballé

Sitting between popular opera and the tradition of rock opera, which Mercury himself propelled, was the *Barcelona* album collaboration with operatic soprano Montserrat Caballé. *Barcelona* is notably different from most other explorations of opera in popular recording cultures because the album is simultaneously in dialogue with both the rock and operatic genres and audiences through the presence of its two lead performers. Caballé was a Spanish operatic *spinto* soprano[2] who was widely considered the leading interpreter of Verdi and Donizetti of her generation, and a successor to Maria Callas (Blyth, 2008). Caballé's presence on the album

---

2   Spinto is an Italian term used to describe vocal timbre with a 'pushed' quality that is 'large enough to sound powerful and incisive in dramatic climaxes' (Jander and Harris, 2016a). The term also indicates particular operatic repertoire in which this vocal quality is necessary for its realisation (Jander and Harris, 2016a).

lent considerable credibility to the project for art music audiences, as her public profile signified the most elite aspects of operatic performance. Mercury too was widely considered the most virtuosic[3] and iconic rock vocalist of his generation (Gilmore and Greene, 2014) who brought Queen's massive international fan base to the collaboration.

The *Barcelona* collaboration eventuated via a 1986 Spanish radio interview in which Mercury declared that the singer he most admired was Caballé (Promane, 2009, p. 141). Mercury and Caballé subsequently met in March 1987 and spent an evening improvising together with producer/arranger/composer Mike Moran. After, Caballé pursued Mercury to formally collaborate with her on a creative project (Promane, 2009, p. 147). The result was the *Barcelona* album, which brought together Mercury's powerful rock vocals with Caballé's soaring voice, over a mix of synth rock and orchestral textures, on what proved to be Mercury's final solo release.[4] Mercury and Caballé kept their collaboration a secret until a televised concert of a performance in Ibiza, Spain, on 29 May 1987, which was intended to celebrate *Barcelona*'s acceptance to host the 1992 Summer Olympic Games (Promane, 2009, p. 159). The title track 'Barcelona' became one of the two official commemorative songs of the Barcelona Olympics. Notably, the other official commemorative song was a popera track entitled 'Amigos Para Siempre' (Lloyd Webber, 1992) performed by (then) music theatre soprano Sarah Brightman and operatic tenor José Carreras. While Mercury died in 1991, a video montage featuring the song opened the televised coverage of the opening ceremony on 25 July 1992.

The *Barcelona* recordings had three pivotal releases. In 1987, after the initial live performance, 'Barcelona' was released and followed by a full album of the same name in 1988. Songs were co-written by Mercury

---

3 Recent acoustic analysis of Mercury's voice confirms the complexity of his vocal devices, encompassing a 37-semitone vocal range (F#2-G5), a 'surprisingly high mean fundamental frequency modulation rate (vibrato) of 7.0 Hz' and subharmonic phonation (Herbst et al., 2016).
4 Despite being a collaboration, *Barcelona* is widely represented as one of Mercury's solo album releases (for example, see Sullivan, 2012). This representation is likely due to Mercury characterising it this way himself: 'I was planning to do my second solo project, and I really did not want to do another album with a bunch of songs. I wanted this to have something different. It had to have another sort of stamp, something that spearheaded the damn thing. Suddenly, "Barcelona" emerged and swallowed me like a tidal-wave' (cited in Promane, 2009, p. 147). This characterisation stuck, as *Barcelona* was one of only two album releases Mercury made outside of Queen during this period, a period in which Mercury was also actively writing with Mike Moran (see Promane, 2009, p. 142). Another factor in this perception could be that Caballé did not contribute to the album's songwriting, whereas Mercury was active as a songwriter and producer of the release.

and Moran (who formally arranged and notated the orchestration) with Caballé contributing vocal cadenzas (Promane, 2009, p. 151). Tracks from *Barcelona* were included in *The Freddie Mercury Album*, a compilation of Mercury's solo repertoire released by EMI in 1992. For the 2012 reissue of *Barcelona*, Stuart Morley reorchestrated the synthesised orchestra parts and they were replaced with recordings by the 80-piece FILMharmonic Orchestra.

Each *Barcelona* release has been met with degrees of scepticism from music critics, mostly reviewing from the rock perspective, who have struggled with the combination of rock and operatic sensibilities. The *Entertainment Weekly* review that opens this chapter was typical of the perplexed responses to *Barcelona*. After contextualising the juxtaposition of Mercury and Caballé as performers, this review cuts to the heart of the difficulty:

> All the material in Barcelona (cowritten by Mercury) is penned in a style meant to snub rock in favor of 'real' opera, but likable pop hooks keep peeking through. The stuff lands somewhere between Andrew Lloyd Webber and 'Climb Ev'ry Mountain.' Such a goofy context ultimately makes Caballé seem less like Maria Callas and more like Yma Sumac. But then, Mercury's reverence for the star and his flair for kitsch make this a novelty item too cracked to resist. (Farber, 1992)

Characterisations of the album, including 'flaky', 'goofy', 'kitsch' and 'novelty' (Farber, 1992), are echoed in reviews of the 2012 re-release, which similarly struggle with the pairing of Mercury and Caballé's voices:

> Possibility [sic] the weirdest combo in pop history: the flamboyant Queen frontman Freddie Mercury and opera superstar Montserrat Caballé certainly hit the world between the eyes with their Barcelona album 25 years ago. To mark its quarter century, this special edition has been reworked … You can tell the difference: big and lush and sweeping, it makes the previous version seem a little on the cheap side. Whether you can handle that eccentric vocal pairing, mind you, is quite another matter. (Gage, 2012)

At some level, these descriptions of *Barcelona* as a 'weird', 'eccentric', 'novelty' project are justified because the pairing of two such iconic operatic and rock virtuosi was something not previously heard within popular recording cultures. However, looking at the project within the trajectory of Mercury's career, the vocal and compositional devices employed in

Barcelona are a logical extension of the playful exploration of operatic forms he had been entertaining since he wrote 'Bohemian Rhapsody'. An analysis of the musical and vocal devices Mercury employed across *Barcelona* and 'Bohemian Rhapsody' establishes the continuity of this trajectory (see Table 7.1). Table 7.1 also compares the vocal devices Caballé employed on repertory opera recordings[5] with her vocal performance on *Barcelona*. Additionally, sonic and musical alterations made for the 2012 reissue of the *Barcelona* album due to its reorchestration by Morley are also noted in Table 7.1. This analysis is used to assess the impact and rationale behind the critical reception of *Barcelona* within popular recording cultures.

An analysis of the *Barcelona* releases and 'Bohemian Rhapsody' compiled for this article is summarised in Table 7.1 and indicates that compositional forms are fairly consistent between 'Bohemian Rhapsody' and the *Barcelona* songs. The aesthetic tendency underpinning both releases is operatic pastiche woven though rock with heavily mediated, hyper-real music production devices including vocal overdubbing and audible effects processing. Such production techniques have frequented Mercury's songwriting and are present in earlier songs such as 'My Fairy King' (1973), which similarly used densely overdubbed vocals to create a choral effect. Mercury's piano playing, familiar to Queen fans from 'Bohemian Rhapsody' and other tracks including 'Nevermore' (1974), 'In the Lap of the Gods' (1974) and 'Love of My Life' (1975), also features in *Barcelona* and is particularly showcased in 'The Fallen Priest'. However, a key sonic difference in *Barcelona* is the absence of electric guitars as an instrumental texture in favour of strings timbres (synthesised in the 1988 album release). Drums are replaced by orchestral percussion except on 'The Golden Boy' and 'How Can I Go On'.

---

5 Sampled recordings include Bellini: Norma (1973), Verdi: Aida (1986) and Donizetti: Lucrezia Borgia (1989).

POPULAR MUSIC, STARS AND STARDOM

Table 7.1: A comparison of vocal, instrumental and production devices in repertory opera, *Barcelona* and 'Bohemian Rhapsody'

Text	Repertory Opera (*bel canto* repertoire as performed by Caballé on recording)	'Bohemian Rhapsody' (1975 single release)	*Barcelona* (1987 performance and 1988 album)	*Barcelona* (2012 album reissue)
Vocal devices				
Vocal ornamentation (including embellished runs, trills, turns and slides)	✓	✓	Mercury: ✓ Caballé: ✓ Frequent ornamentation throughout Caballé's performance, particularly in the form of elaborate cadenzas	Mercury: ✓ Caballé: ✓ Frequent ornamentation throughout Caballé's performance, particularly in the form of elaborate cadenzas
Wide vocal range for lead performer (2.5+ octaves)	✓	✓	Mercury: ✓ Caballé: ✓	Mercury: ✓ Caballé: ✓
Vocal chorus (defined as layered, multi-part accompanying vocals including vocal overdubbing)	Chorus and ensemble singing: ✓	Backup singers: ✓ Vocal overdubbing: ✓	Backup singers: ✓ Vocal overdubbing: ✓	Backup singers: ✓ Vocal overdubbing: ✓
Speech-level vocalities/devices (including belting, yelling, talking and intoned-speech inflections)	Rarely used	✓	Mercury: ✓ Caballé: ✗	Mercury: ✓ Caballé: ✗
Legato phrase shaping	✓	✓	Mercury: ✓ Caballé: ✓	Mercury: ✓ Caballé: ✓

7. WHEN DIVAS AND ROCK STARS COLLIDE

Text	Repertory Opera (bel canto repertoire as performed by Caballé on recording)	'Bohemian Rhapsody' (1975 single release)	Barcelona (1987 performance and 1988 album)	Barcelona (2012 album reissue)
Accented vocal effects (including glottal stops, marked/accented notes)	✓	✓	Mercury: ✓ Caballé: ✓	Mercury: ✓ Caballé: ✓
Vocal vibrato	✓	Present on sustained notes	Mercury: ✓ Present throughout on sustained notes but utilised more frequently in classically oriented songs particularly 'Ensueño' and 'La Japonaise' Caballé: ✓	Mercury: ✓ Present throughout on sustained notes but utilised more frequently in classically oriented songs particularly 'Ensueño' and 'La Japonaise' Caballé: ✓
Amplified vocal textures (including breath sounds, rasps and whispering)	Rarely used	✓	Mercury: ✓ Caballé: ✗ Microphone employed for amplification but not utilised to inflect vocal production	Mercury: ✓ Caballé: ✗ Microphone employed for amplification but not utilised to inflect vocal production
Performance languages	Various	English	English, Japanese, Spanish	English, Japanese, Spanish
Timbral complexity (complex overtones present in vocal tone)	High	Moderate (Mercury)	Caballé: High Mercury: Moderate	Caballé: High Mercury: Moderate

125

Text	Repertory Opera (bel canto repertoire as performed by Caballé on recording)	'Bohemian Rhapsody' (1975 single release)	Barcelona (1987 performance and 1988 album)	Barcelona (2012 album reissue)
Instrumentation				
Dense orchestration/instrumentation	✓	✓	✓	✓
Orchestral instrument timbres	✓	✗	Synthesised orchestral instruments dominate recorded version. A combination of synthesisers and live performers used in the Ibiza performance	Synthesisers replaced with orchestral accompaniment
Electronic and rock instrument timbres	✗	✓	✓ Most notably used in 'The Golden Boy' and 'How Can I Go On'. No electric guitars present	✓ Most notably used in 'The Golden Boy' and 'How Can I Go On'. No electric guitars present
Musical structure	Varied and complex. Often featuring through-composition. Typically encompass instrumental interludes, chorus, aria, recitative and ensemble sections	Varied and complex. Featuring through-composition, instrumental and vocal solos, overdubbed chorus parts, ensemble parts, and recitative-like sectional joins	Various structural devices employed. Complex but some tracks oriented around song forms particularly in singles released from the album. Also features instrumental and vocal solos, overdubbed chorus parts, ensemble parts, and recitative-like sectional joins	Various structural devices employed. Complex but some tracks oriented around song forms particularly in singles released from the album. Also features instrumental and vocal solos, overdubbed chorus parts, ensemble parts, and recitative-like sectional joins

7. WHEN DIVAS AND ROCK STARS COLLIDE

Text	Repertory Opera (bel canto repertoire as performed by Caballé on recording)	'Bohemian Rhapsody' (1975 single release)	Barcelona (1987 performance and 1988 album)	Barcelona (2012 album reissue)
Production devices				
Inclusion of audible production effects and processing	✗	✓	✓	✓
Mix spatialisation	Mediated but transparent	Heavily mediated and noticeably manipulated	Heavily mediated and noticeably manipulated	Mediated and noticeably manipulated – particularly evident on Mercury's vocals
Live performance amplification	Used occasionally and discreetly	✓	✓	N/A

127

The inclusion of synthesised orchestral parts in the 1988 *Barcelona* release occupies a kind of timbral middle ground, pointing towards classical music's orchestral colours, while retaining timbral associations more familiar to popular releases of the period. When synthesisers are replaced by orchestral recordings in the 2012 release, the feel of the record shifts towards classical music. Two factors influence this aesthetic reorientation. First, the orchestral recordings have been produced with a transparent, 'naturalistic' balance typical of classical music recordings[6] whereby instruments are placed in a fixed location within the mix and clarity between instruments is emphasised. Second, when Mercury's voice—processed, layered and occasionally panned in different locations—is added to these parts, these production devices can sound over-emphasised because the treatment remains distinct from everything else in the mix. Therefore, the electronic synthesiser timbres in the 1998 release act as a kind of kludge, keeping timbral associations between classical and popular music in balance.

While 'Bohemian Rhapsody' appropriated opera irreverently, *Barcelona* is much more of an homage. This is partly due to Caballé's imposing vocal presence, but also because operatic devices are developed more carefully and accompanied by orchestral instrumentation. One example is the 'Ensueño' duet, which incorporates solos highlighting Caballé's *bel canto*[7] vocal technique through sustained legato phrases. Mercury sings with markedly more classical inflections on 'Ensueño' by restricting the range of speech-level vocal devices, maintaining a more consistently lyric tone and incorporating more vibrato than is typical for his singing. Beyond rock and opera, *Barcelona* features an eclectic range of influences, with Mercury and Moran incorporating elements of gospel into 'The Golden Boy', and a flagrant exoticisation of Japanese traditional music in 'La Japonaise'.

---

6   See Klein (2014), Blake (2012, pp. 4611–4621).
7   *Bel Canto* is an Italian term for 'beautiful singing'. Stark (2011, p. xvii) considers that it is a term in search of meaning because it connotes 'many aspects of vocal history and pedagogy including several "golden ages" of singing, a number of specific techniques of voice production, and a variety of stylistic vocal idioms'. In the context of this article, the term *bel canto* is employed with a general usage application defined by Jander and Harris (2016b) as referring to 'the Italian vocal style of the 18th and early 19th centuries, the qualities of which include perfect legato production throughout the range, the use of a light tone in the higher registers and agile and flexible delivery. More narrowly, it is sometimes applied exclusively to Italian opera of the time of Rossini, Bellini and Donizetti. In either case, "bel canto" is usually set in opposition to the development of a weightier, more powerful and speech-inflected style associated with German opera and Wagner in particular'.

Structurally, *Barcelona* experiments with form and utilises through-composition. However, the single releases ('Barcelona' [1987], 'The Golden Boy' [1988] and 'How Can I Go On' [1989]) anchor themselves in popular music by incorporating verses and choruses along with repeated hooks to create points of interest. Operatic devices including recitative, aria and more complex orchestration are incorporated most prominently on the album-only tracks. Notably, 'Overture Piccante', which ends *Barcelona*, mimics the overture by drawing together key themes from each of the preceding album tracks. However, its location at the end of the album, rather than the beginning as would be typical in opera, is more reflective of a climactic rock concert finale, drawing together the most exciting musical themes for a grand finish.

Vocally, Mercury and Caballé exemplify virtuosity in their respective styles, demonstrating extremely wide vocal ranges, embellished vocal ornamentation, accented articulations, legato, huge dynamic variation and complex vocal colouration. Typical of operatic repertoire, the pair also sing in multiple languages: English, Spanish and Japanese. However, while Mercury seems to shift his vocal production more towards classical singing in 'Ensueño', 'La Japonaise' and (to a lesser extent) 'Guide Me Home', Caballé never compromises her classical technique.[8] This means that despite microphones being employed to capture her voice, she does not utilise their possibilities for producing more intimate, speech-oriented vocal qualities. In the recording context, Mercury's performance reads as more nuanced than Caballé's because he employs every available vocal device towards wordpainting. Potter (1998, pp. 188–198) concurs with this analysis, considering Mercury's delivery 'much more dynamic' because Mercury 'does not have the ideological baggage of several hundred years to restrain him'. Additionally, Caballé's operatic vocal production, with elongated vowels, minimised consonants and emphasised vibrato, serves to blur English language lyrics to the extent that they frequently become unintelligible and the listener must rely upon Mercury's repetitions of text for meaning. The effect of this is to make Mercury the interpreter of Caballé's exotic and otherworldly voice. Despite this, the virtuosic command and mutual respect each singer demonstrates throughout *Barcelona* implies that they have reached a kind of equivalency or

---

8   Promane cites Moran as saying that Mercury and Caballé deliberately chose to maintain their distinct vocal techniques, and not swap vocal traditions for *Barcelona* (1992, p. 170). However, while not abandoning his rock vocality, Mercury modifies his vocal production for expressivity in certain *Barcelona* tracks, which brings their quality more in line with classical vocalities.

equilibrium between their respective vocalities. The metaphorical distance between rock and operatic singing seems very small when two such voices are paired.

Conclusion: Colliding Genres, Ruptured Authenticities

With *Barcelona,* two global superstars collaborated by bringing their divergent vocalities and musical traditions into dialogue. However, as icons of their respective genres, Mercury and Caballé were also asking their individual audiences to bridge a wide cultural and historical gulf that existed between opera and rock, or elite and popular music more broadly. In simple terms, Scott describes authentic music as 'the music that has the effect of making you believe in its truthfulness', a truthfulness that may be an 'assemblage of signs governed by conventions' (2009, pp. 3–4). Rock and opera construct authenticity in different ways, employing vastly different, and somewhat opposing, lexicons of signs that are received and ascribed meaning and value by their audiences. To understand how authenticities circulate across these two genres, we need to unpack the concept of authenticity as it might play out for the respective audiences, at the level of interpretation. Moore (2002) proposes a framework of authenticity that operates at three distinct yet interacting perspectives, which he describes as first-, second- and third-person authenticity. First-person authenticity, as an 'authenticity of expression', occurs when a composer or performer 'succeeds in conveying the impression that his/her utterance is one of integrity, that it represents an attempt to communicate in an unmediated form with an audience' (Moore, 2002, p. 214). Second-person authenticity, as an 'authenticity of experience', occurs when 'a performance succeeds in conveying the impression to a listener that that listener's experience of life is being validated, that the music is "telling it like it is" for them' (Moore, 2002, p. 220). Third-person authenticity, as an 'authenticity of execution', occurs when 'a performer succeeds in conveying the impression of accurately representing the ideas of another, embedded within a tradition of performance', such as successful reinterpretation of traditional music, or tribute band performances (Moore, 2002, p. 218). Through this model, Moore constructs a notion of authenticity, not as an embedded musical trait, but rather as something born of interpretation, 'which is made and fought for from within a cultural and, thus, historicised position' (2002, p. 210).

To interpret *Barcelona*, we must consider the respective cultural and historicised position of the release within the milieus of rock and opera. McLeod (2001, p. 189) writes that rock has 'traditionally resisted opera, a genre seemingly steeped in the divisions of class and high culture which rock music, ostensibly, rejects'. McLeod also notes that:

> The audience and fans of each genre are often highly immobile in their tastes and often deeply suspicious—even resentful—of the opposing form. In broadly general terms, fans of rock music typically find opera to be highly contrived, confusing and convoluted, boring, elitist and arcane, while opera fans typically resent the perceived musical simplicity, loudness, commerciality and banality of rock music. (p. 189)

In the context of *Barcelona*, McLeod's observations are particularly apt. Mercury's virtuosic vocal style and approach to songwriting is not markedly changed from 'Bohemian Rhapsody', marking a consistency in expression across his performances. However, Caballé's presence in the *Barcelona* project renders *Barcelona* inauthentic for rock audiences because it made clear the correlation between Mercury's musical proclivities and the operatic tradition, rupturing a distance that audiences may have preferred to keep separate. Her presence on the album, noted by rock reviewers as an oddity or, in the most extreme review, a 'con' (Farber, 1992), seems impossible to reconcile for critics and audiences familiar with Mercury's Queen releases, thereby affecting their reception of its expression and experience. Applying Moore's authenticity schema to this perspective reveals that in utilising a genuine operatic diva and by replacing guitars with an orchestra, the performance and aesthetics became too clearly aligned with opera for *Barcelona* to validate an experience of rock culture, or communicate with immediacy and integrity to a rock audience. Similarly, Caballé's audiences were familiar with her as an exemplar exponent of *bel canto* repertory opera. However, in *Barcelona*, Caballé's voice often occupied an accompanying role to Mercury and her vocal parts were simple compared to those in her operatic roles because of the condensed song format of the album. This brings her performance more in line with popera recordings, which tend to simplify and shorten arrangements of operatic repertoire while retaining operatic vocal timbre. Classical reviewers have equally struggled with this apparent simplicity, with Hensher (2006) commenting:

Barcelona may sound 'operatic', but it is only a three-minute song of banging and crashing—all climax and no crescendo. Some of Wagner's single musical structures last over two hours—and no rock musician has a clue how to start constructing something like that.

Applying Moore's authenticity schema to the operatic perspective, the failure of the *Barcelona* recording with classical critics leads back to embedded notions of how opera should be executed. Mercury and Moran's composition and Cabellé's vocal performance were too simplistic to effectively execute a rendering of opera that was palatable for its aficionados.

Ultimately, to understanding critical responses to *Barcelona*, we must consider the work in relation to its audiences, and move beyond a consideration of the musical outcomes and the artistic contributions of its lead performers. Despite the collaboration being original, despite both performers contributing virtuosic vocal performances and despite the music continuing a songwriting trajectory Mercury had commenced earlier in his career, *Barcelona* was received with a degree of incredulity by both serious rock and operatic critics. Though *Barcelona* sounds like a collision of opera and rock due to Mercury and Moran's grandiose and eclectic songwriting, it *feels* too much like crossover music for opera and rock critics to find it palatable. Consequently, *Barcelona*'s reception has struggled because it antagonises multiple authenticity gaps between operatic and rock performance styles that have been rigorously maintained throughout the twentieth century by aficionados of both genres. This implies a larger struggle of execution, whereby each genre is effectively signified, but in ways that render both traditions of performance as inauthentic. Each genre has its own aesthetic, performative, cultural and social functions that generate value, but these were called into question when the two artists occupied the same creative space. Mercury and Caballé's individual stardom was so great that the achievements of the *Barcelona* recordings struggle for traction against the genre cultures and iconographies each artist represented individually—the presence of the other de-authenticates the musical experience for their respective audiences. The pinnacle of their particular vocal and musical worlds, Mercury and Caballé's collaboration is problematic precisely because it bridged the popular–elite divide from both directions simultaneously.

References

Adorno, T. 1990. 'Opera and the Long-Playing Record'. *October* 55 (Winter): 62–66. jstor.org/stable/778937 (accessed 3 March 2016).

ARIA. 2016. 'End of Year Charts'. aria.com.au/pages/aria-charts-end-of-year-charts.htm (accessed 14 March 2016).

Ashby, A. 2010. *Absolute Music, Mechanical Reproduction* (Kindle Edition). California: University of California Press. doi.org/10.1525/california/9780520264793.001.0001

Bessette, R. L. 1999. *Mario Lanza: Tenor in Exile*. Portland: Amadeus Press.

Blake, A. 2012. 'Simulating the Ideal Performance: Suvi Raj Grubb and Classical Music Production'. In *The Art of Record Production: An Introductory Reader for a New Academic Field* (Kindle Edition), edited by S. Frith and S. Zagorski-Thomas. Farnham: Ashgate Publishing.

Blyth, A. 2008. 'Caballé, Montserrat'. In *The Grove Book of Opera Singers* (2nd ed.), edited by L. Macy. Oxford: Oxford University Press.

Day, T. 2000. *A Century of Recorded Music: Listening to Musical History*. New Haven: Yale University Press.

Discogs.com. 2016. 'Mario Lanza'. discogs.com/artist/454852-Mario-Lanza?filter_anv=0&subtype=Singles-EPs&type=Releases (accessed 24 March 2016).

Dolezal, R. and H. Rossacher. 2000. *Freddie Mercury, the Untold Story*. UK: Arte/DoRo Produktion/ZDF.

Farber, J. 1992. 'Barcelona'. *Entertainment Weekly*, 7 August. ew.com/article/1992/08/07/music-review-barcelona (accessed 22 February 2016).

Gage, S. 2012. 'CD Review: Freddie Mercury and Montserrat Caballé: Barcelona'. *Express*, 31 August. express.co.uk/entertainment/music/343023/Cd-Review-Freddie-Mercury-and-Montserr-at-Caball-Barcelona (accessed 20 March 2012).

Gilmore, M. and A. Greene. 2014. 'Queen's Tragic Rhapsody'. *Rolling Stone* 1212 (1213): 77–83.

Hensher, P. 2006. 'C Sharp? What's C Sharp?'. *The Guardian*, 26 October. theguardian.com/music/2006/oct/26/classicalmusicandopera.popandrock (accessed 22 March 2016).

Herbst, C., S. Hertegard, D. Zangger-Borch and P. A. Lindestad. 2016. 'Freddie Mercury—Acoustic Analysis of Speaking Fundamental Frequency, Vibrato, and Subharmonics'. *Logopedics Phoniatrics Vocology* 42 (1): 29–38. doi.org/10.3109/14015439.2016.1156737

Hischak, T. 2009. 'Lanza, Mario'. *The Oxford Companion to the American Musical*. oxfordreference.com/view/10.1093/acref/9780195335330.001.0001/acref-9780195335330-e-1032 (accessed 22 February 2016).

Jander, O. and E. T. Harris. 2016a. 'Spinto'. Grove Music Online. doi.org/10.1093/gmo/9781561592630.article.26428

———. 2016b. 'Bel Canto'. Grove Music Online. doi.org/10.1093/gmo/9781561592630.article.02551

Klein, E. 2013. 'Alien Divas and Sampled Sirens: A Brief Mapping of Opera in Popular Music From 1980–2005'. In *Shifting Sounds: Musical Flow—A Collection of Papers from the 2012 IASPM Australia/New Zealand Conference*, edited by O. Wilson and S. Attfield, 106–16. Dunedin: International Association for the Study of Popular Music, Australia and New Zealand Branch.

———. 2014. 'Is Classical Music "Boring"? A Discussion of Fidelity, Virtuosity and Performance in Classical Music Recording'. In *Popular Music Communities, Places and Ecologies: IASPM–ANZ Conference 2013*, edited by J. O'Regan and T. Wren, 112–25. Brisbane: International Association for the Study of Popular Music, Australia and New Zealand Branch.

Lockheart, P. 2003. 'A History of Early Microphone Singing, 1925–1939: American Mainstream Popular Singing at the Advent of Electronic Microphone Amplification'. *Popular Music and Society* 26 (3): 367–385. doi.org/10.1080/0300776032000117003

Macy, L. 2009. 'Caruso, Enrico'. In *The Grove Book of Opera Singers* (2nd ed.), edited by L. Macy. Oxford: Oxford University Press.

McLeod, K. 2001. 'Bohemian Rhapsodies: Operatic Influences on Rock Music'. *Popular Music* 20 (2): 189–203. doi.org/10.1017/S0261143001001404

Moore, A. 2002. 'Authenticity as Authentication'. *Popular Music* 21 (2): 209–223. doi.org/10.1017/S0261143002002131

Morton, D. 1999. *Off the Record: The Technology and Culture of Sound Recording in America* (Kindle edition). New Jersey: Rutgers University Press.

Philip, R. 2004. *Performing Music in the Age of Recording*. New Haven: Yale University Press.

Potter, J. 1998. *Vocal Authority: Singing Style and Ideology*. Cambridge: Cambridge University Press. doi.org/10.1017/CBO9780511470226

Potter, J. and N. Sorrell. 2012. *A History of Singing*. Cambridge: Cambridge University Press. doi.org/10.1017/CBO9781139024419

Promane, B. 2009. 'Freddie Mercury and Queen: Technologies of Genre and the Poetics of Innovation', unpublished PhD thesis, University of Western Ontario, London.

Scott, D. 2009. 'Introduction'. In *The Ashgate Research Companion to Popular Musicology*, edited by D. Scott. Farnham: Ashgate Publishing. doi.org/10.2307/j.ctt4cgjnm.4

Stark, J. 2011. *Bel Canto: A History of Vocal Pedagogy*. Toronto: University of Toronto Press.

Sullivan, C. 2012. 'Freddie Mercury: The Great Enigma'. *The Guardian*, 28 September. theguardian.com/music/2012/sep/27/freddie-mercury-great-enigma (accessed 17 October 2016).

Thorpe, R. (Director). 1951. *The Great Caruso*. USA: Metro-Goldwyn-Mayer.

Whiteley, S. 2011. 'Mercury, Freddie'. In *Oxford Dictionary of National Biography* (Online edition). Oxford: Oxford University Press. doi.org/10.1093/ref:odnb/49895

8
Intimacy, Authenticity and 'Worlding' in Beyoncé's Star Project

Phoebe Macrossan

At the 2014 MTV Video Music Awards, African-American pop star Beyoncé Knowles-Carter (known professionally as Beyoncé) performed a 12-song medley from her self-titled visual album, *Beyoncé* (2013), recreating its imagery across moving stages, treadmills, giant screens and a large troupe of dancers. To open this typically large-scale performance, she said, 'MTV, welcome to my world'. This choice of words is interesting because, as a dominant figure in the popular music scene, Beyoncé hardly need introduce herself. What this moment captures, however, is the increasing personal intimacy of Beyoncé's stardom, and her transition to the active creation and ownership of an identifiable, holistic 'world'. This chapter argues that Beyoncé's stardom extends beyond constructing a star image through media texts (Dyer, 1998, p. 10). I argue that her star project, her ongoing construction and maintenance of her stardom is creating an intimate, identifiable, holistic world: 'Beyoncé World'. I use the term 'star project' because there is no beginning, middle and end as suggested by a term like 'star narrative', and because worlding is more encompassing and widespread than the term 'star image' put forward by Richard Dyer (1998, p. 10), although it is a continuation of it.

Beyoncé World is created and maintained primarily through Beyoncé's music videos and visual albums, but also across her concerts, performances and public appearances, and her social media accounts and website. Therefore, Beyoncé World is primarily created through media images, but, importantly, it also includes public appearances, actions and performances outside these visual images. Worlding includes both the active process of creating a world and the world itself. Creating Beyoncé World is Beyoncé's entire performance of stardom. Beyoncé World has geography, both specific and nondescript, it has 'real' people and characters, a past, present and a future, and it has a political ideology on race, sex and gender that aligns with Beyoncé's outward public statements and past musical career. The 2014 VMA performance is not the first instance of her worlding, but it is a noteworthy public acknowledgement of a strategy that continues today.

Beyoncé is a significant subject for star studies, not only for her huge commercial and artistic achievements.[1] This chapter argues that Beyoncé's worlding represents new articulations of stardom and authenticity previously unaccounted for in the contemporary media landscape. 'Authenticity' is a widely contested term in popular music studies, but it is still relevant to discussions of stardom because of how the concept is actively used by pop stars and their fans. As Su Holmes and Sean Redmond (2006, p. 4) argue, 'fandom, and the construction of stars and celebrities, has always involved the "search" for the "authentic" person that lies behind the manufactured mask of fame'. Other contemporary pop stars construct an 'authentic' star image through sharing intimate details of their lives via social media or semiautobiographical albums and music videos. Beyoncé's construction of Beyoncé World, however, is more extensive, widespread, complex, layered, controlled and consistent, and requires further scrutiny.

This chapter examines the construction of Beyoncé World within her recent artistic output, the one-hour long visual album *Lemonade* (Knowles-Carter 2016a). *Lemonade* is a concept visual album that focuses on a relationship marred by infidelity. Like *Beyoncé* before it, *Lemonade* was a surprise release that caused much discussion of its aesthetics, themes,

---

1   At the time of writing, Beyoncé has sold more than 86.1 million albums as a solo artist and 58.6 million with girl group Destiny's Child. She is the most nominated woman in Grammy Awards history with 63 nominations, of which she has won 22. She has also won 24 MTV Video Music Awards, the most of any artist in history. As of June 2017, her net worth was US$350 million. See Jones (2016) and Forbes (2017).

politics and subject matter. *Lemonade* is the most significant example to date of Beyoncé worlding. It is also in conversation with, and adds to the world created through, her past albums, videos, social media accounts and website. As *Lemonade* premiered as a 60-minute film on US cable television network HBO, it is also a prime example of a star using filmic techniques to promote an album. Thus, it is a pertinent example of how film theory can be applied to popular music performance.

To consider Beyoncé World, I use theories of worlding and worldhood developed in film theory. To this end, I borrow V. F. Perkins' (2005) ideas of 'worlding' and 'worldhood', which are constructed by elements of film style (camera angles, editing, acting, etc.). I also borrow from Daniel Yacavone's (2015, p. 9) concept of the 'film world', which is a 'singular, holistic, relational, and fundamentally referential reality' that possesses sensory, symbolic and affective dimensions for the audience. Film (or music video) worlds are identifiable worlds separate from our own, but connected to it through a borrowing process (Yacavone, 2015, p. 20). The audience understands the constructed nature of the world, but can relate it to the so-called 'real' world by extension. This accounts for how Beyoncé's worlding is achieved by both her artistic and professional output (videos, concerts, media images, appearances, etc.) and the audience's knowledge of, immersion and participation in her worlding. While film theory has been usefully employed by popular music studies to concentrate on the formal aspects of music video—to examine their stylistic elements, and narrative or non-narrative status, for example—theories of film worlds have yet to be utilised.[2] As many scholars have noted, music videos are the primary texts for selling a musician and their music. Doing this usually means aligning the music video's imagery with the artist's brand. Most music video scholars argue the form is non-narrative, at least in the classical Hollywood cinematic sense (Vernallis, 2004, p. 3). Instead, Carol Vernallis (2004, p. 13) argues music videos focus on foregrounding the song's form rather than telling a story. While Beyoncé's music videos do display semi-narrative and episodic traits, they are better understood as part of a larger whole that is her star project: constructing and maintaining

---

2   Key texts in music video scholarship include E. Ann Kaplan's *Rocking Around the Clock* (1987), Andrew Goodwin's *Dancing in the Distraction Factory* (1992), *Sound and Vision* (1993), edited by Simon Frith, Andrew Goodwin and Lawrence Grossberg, *Medium Cool* (2007), edited by Roger Beebe and Jason Middleton, and *Experiencing Music Video* (2004) by Carol Vernallis. The first wave of discussion was largely spurred by the launch of MTV on cable television in the US in 1981. These texts analyse music videos across a range of areas: their formal properties, genres, stylistic elements, representational politics and practices, and their transmedia status. For a discussion of music video foregrounding song form and performance, see Frith (1996, pp. 224–225) and Vernallis (2004, p. 4).

Beyoncé World. Understanding music videos as part of a star's worlding practices can illuminate how music videos are not isolated performance texts or dreamscapes loosely connected to a star, but form part of a larger universe actively created and inhabited by them.

This chapter will first examine the worlding techniques of film style and audience immersion in *Lemonade*, and the properties that make up Beyoncé World. It will then consider the significance of worlding to Beyoncé's larger star project. It is important to stress here that Yacavone (2008, p. 84) argues that cinematic works create and present *a* world, rather than fictional narratives or representations of *the* world. Beyoncé World is a distinct and separate world from our own, but it is informed and enhanced by its connections to persons and relationships of the real world.

Lemonade

Beyoncé is as yet the only major pop star to release visual albums, and her decision to do so represents her understanding of the contemporary media environment.[3] By premiering *Lemonade* first on HBO on 23 April 2016, and later releasing it for download on Tidal and iTunes, Beyoncé turned her album release into an event, guaranteed to be watched by a captive television audience, then downloaded by dedicated fans both within and outside the US who may have missed the broadcast. The surprise release also generates publicity of its own accord through its unexpectedness, thereby driving sales in a saturated market. By simultaneously releasing the music and visuals, she ensured the interpretation of her music and stardom visually and aurally in one cohesive unit. In a promotional video for her self-titled album, Beyoncé detailed the motivations behind releasing a visual album in one digital drop:

> I see music. It's more than just what I hear ... Now people only listen to a few seconds of a song on their iPods. They don't really invest in a whole album ... I wanted everyone to see the whole picture, and to see how personal everything is to me ... There's so much that gets between the music, the artist, and the fans. I felt like I didn't want anybody to give the message when my record is coming out. I just want this to come out when it's ready and from me to my fans.[4]

---

3 While I acknowledge that it is difficult to attribute these business decisions entirely to pop stars themselves, Beyoncé is a special case in that, since 2010, she has been self-managed. See Kennedy (2011).
4 Beyoncé interviewed in Heinzerling (2013).

We can assume these intentions also apply to *Lemonade*, given it was released in a similar way. Releasing a long visual album intended to be watched in one sitting fits the binge-watching culture enabled by digital download and streaming technologies of music, film and television. Beyoncé's statement that fans can 'see how personal everything is to me' and that the album flows 'from me to my fans' also reflects the ethos of the web 2.0 environment. Social media technologies such as Facebook, Twitter, Instagram and YouTube mean that a perceived direct means of communication exists between celebrities and fans. Beyoncé is playing to this idea when she digitally 'drops' her visual albums; the action is like file-sharing between friends.

Aside from its digital visual album format, a large part of the popular discourse on *Lemonade* focused on how it engages with the Black Lives Matter movement and its celebration of black women and black female sexuality.[5] Much scholarship on Beyoncé discusses her negotiation of body, race and gender politics, and how this contributes to her identity as an African-American female pop star.[6] *Lemonade* continues Beyoncé's negotiation of race, sexuality and gender, as it features many references to African-American women and Southern history, particularly black female identity, sexuality, spirituality, as well as witchcraft, menstruation, slavery and African Yoruba culture and religion. Theories of worlding illuminate how the complex interplay between these themes and multi-layered intertextual references make up the stylised world of *Lemonade*. Yacavone (2012, p. 36) argues that fictional representation and narrative, together with film sound and music, account for the created and experienced totality of a film's presentation, or what he terms the 'film world'. These elements then combine with the audience's own experience of the real world:

> To make a film is also to construct a world. As viewers, we are invited to enter into this world, to share it with its maker(s) and with other viewers. When made, experienced, and understood as art, the virtual worlds of films, including all narrative ones, not only provide a form of experience that approaches in many ways our actual, embodied life experience but also mediates it in aesthetic ways, sometimes to powerful cognitive and affective ends. (Yacavone, 2015, p. 9)

---

5   See, for example, Clark (2016), Lockett, Weatherford and Peoples (2016) and Oluo (2016).
6   See, for example, James (2008), Griffin (2011), Durham (2012), Weidhase (2015) and Chatman (2015), and the anthology *The Beyoncé Effect: Essays on Sexuality, Race and Feminism* (2016), edited by Adrienne Trier-Bieniek.

Using Yacavone's logic, *Lemonade* creates Beyoncé World not just through its camera angles, editing, costuming and staging, or the loose story it narrates of an adulterous marriage, but through extra-narrative elements and the affective qualities that connect to the audience's own lived experience. These include musical choices such as genre, vocal style, pitch, tone, timbre and rhythm, textual intertitles and spoken poetry that frame each song, and the multitude of intertextual references to both Beyoncé World created outside *Lemonade* and the viewer's own 'real' world.[7] *Lemonade*'s representations of black womanhood encourage the audience to make connections to Beyoncé's history of engagement with feminism and black female empowerment.[8] The most public acknowledgements of Beyoncé's politics pre-*Lemonade* are her 2014 VMA performance—in which she sampled a speech from feminist author Chimamanda Ngozi Adichie while standing in front of a projection of the word 'FEMINIST'— and her 2016 Superbowl performance of the song 'Formation'—in which she made reference to the Black Lives Matter movement, Malcolm X and the Black Panthers. While one cannot assume every consumer of *Lemonade* would be familiar with these moments, they did generate significant public reporting and commentary in the mainstream press.[9]

Lemonade begins with a montage of seemingly unconnected images: a close-up of Beyoncé kneeling in front of a car; an extreme low-angle black-and-white shot of a chain hanging from the trees above; and a forward-pushing long shot of historic Fort Macomb in Louisiana. The camera cuts to a medium long shot of Beyoncé kneeling in front of a red curtain on a lit stage as she sings the opening lines of the first song, 'Pray You Catch Me'. This is intercut with shots of her walking though the long grass at Fort Macomb. The stage signals the beginning of a representation of Beyoncé's life, her inner thoughts and journeys, her vulnerability of baring herself in the spotlight, but also the theatrical and fictional elements of the film. This artificiality does not negate *Lemonade*'s worldhood;

---

7   Somali-British poet Warsan Shire wrote the poetry read by Beyoncé in *Lemonade*.
8   For a discussion of the questions of race, sex, gender and feminism raised by Beyoncé, see Trier-Bierniek (2016).
9   These political statements by Beyoncé were not universally applauded. Pop star Annie Lennox called it 'feminist lite' (Azzopardi, 2014), and feminist activist and scholar bell hooks described Beyoncé as 'anti-feminist' (Sieczkowski, 2014). Others, such as Durham et al. (2013), were more positive and argue Beyoncé is a hip-hop feminist. For some critics, Beyoncé's engagement with black political activism is problematised by her status as mass commercial product. Ajamu Baraka (2016) called 'Formation' a 'commodified caricature of black opposition', while Dianca London (2016) argued 'her brand of feminism … is severely limited, and her latest activism via "Formation" feels more like strategic consumerist dramatism rather than empowerment'.

as Perkins (2005, p. 38) argues, just because 'the world is created in our imaginations it need not suffer damage from any foregrounding of the devices that assist its construction'.

Lemonade's world exists within the Southern US, one that draws on real places and traditions of the area, but also incorporates elements of fantasy and performance common in music video. Much of the film contains images of typically Southern locations and imagery such as Louisiana plantation houses and accompanying slave quarters, bayous, Southern live oak trees with their hanging moss, the New Orleans Mercedes-Benz Superdome and Fort Macomb. Beyoncé and her dancers are often dressed in antebellum style, particularly during the songs 'Freedom' and 'Formation'. This world of the South, then, is at once anachronistic, fantastical and utopian; the plantation houses are largely occupied by black women who sing, dance, climb trees and eat together while white slave owners are nowhere on the scene. Beyoncé's African, Creole and Native American heritage, and Texan upbringing, are frequently referred to in the lyrics and visuals. There are also more urban locations, such as the city streets in the songs 'Hold Up' and '6 Inch', the underground carpark in 'Don't Hurt Yourself', and the images of a flooded New Orleans and a small boy dancing in front of a line of riot police in 'Formation'.

Beyoncé World is built up through the connections between these spaces, by layering on the visual references, lyrical and musical cues and building on her past and present political engagement.[10] This world is a distinctly black female space, where women of Beyoncé's immediate family, but also prominent black women, are celebrated. Her friends and family consistently appear in cameo, as do other notable African-American women: tennis star Serena Williams, musician Zendaya, actresses Quvenzhané Wallis and Amandla Stenberg, and model Winnie Harlow, among others. *Lemonade* also features the mothers of slain black men who have become the face of the Black Lives Matter movement: Sybrina Fulton, mother of Trayvon Martin; Lezley McSpadden, mother of Michael Brown; and Gwen Carr, mother of Eric Garner. This political engagement connects with her statements in support of Black Lives Matter during her concerts and on her website.[11] The connection of these individuals to the 'real' world adds to the worlding practices of *Lemonade*. This connection to reality,

---

10   Perrott, Rogers and Vernallis (2016) provide an excellent breakdown of the visual references and connections between sound and image in *Lemonade*.
11   See Knowles-Carter (2016b).

to a 'real' person on the other side of the camera, sharing the space of the viewer, enhances the worldhood of the film through the borrowing process (Yacavone, 2015, p. 20).

Beyoncé's direct address to the camera, a staple of television and music video, but less common in feature-length film, does not detract from the worlding of *Lemonade*. In fact, it enhances it. Perkins (2005, p. 36) states, 'When I respond to the invitation of the outward glance I engage in the fiction in a new way, by imagining contact rather than separation between my world and the screen world'. The implied addressee is at once a character in the film, but also Beyoncé's husband: rapper, producer and businessman Shawn Carter (known professionally as Jay-Z). Jay-Z is a real-life figure who exists both within Beyoncé World in *Lemonade*, as he appears in songs 'Sandcastles' and 'All Night', and outside, in the 'real' world, in his professional life. Worlding 'works for an audience that knows the world always to be larger and larger again than the sector currently in view' (Perkins, 2005, p. 33). The viewer interpolates the boundaries of the *Lemonade* world as enmeshing with Beyoncé's own 'real' world outside the film—that world they see through social media. In fact, Beyoncé's worlding strategies rely on the intimate and personal nature of the content. The next section considers the connections between the world constructed in *Lemonade* and Beyoncé's stardom.

Worlding and Beyoncé's Star Project

This chapter argues that Beyoncé's stardom extends beyond constructing a star image through media texts (Dyer, 1998, p. 10). Instead, I argue, her star project, her ongoing construction and maintenance of her stardom is creating Beyoncé World. Beyoncé's worlding strategy, as I have suggested, relies heavily on incorporating intimate details of her life. However, this has not always been the case. Early in her career, Beyoncé rarely spoke about her personal life and adopted the stage persona 'Sasha Fierce' to perform her more sexually explicit songs.[12] In 2010, Beyoncé became self-managed, splitting from her father who was her manager from when she was a child. From this point, her albums, videos and interviews became more explicit, personal and intimate, and she lost the stage persona Sasha

---

12 'Sasha Fierce' was introduced with the release of the *I Am ... Sasha Fierce* (2008) album (see Kennedy, 2011).

Fierce. In 2012, she joined Twitter and Instagram and debuted her official website with the tag line 'the official view into my world—by me, for you X B'. In 2013, she released the *Beyoncé* visual album, and a self-directed documentary, *Beyoncé: Life is but a Dream*. Both detailed the split from her father, her marriage, her sexual fantasies, her miscarriage, her relationship with her mother and sister, the birth of her first child and her ambition as an artist. Since 2013, this level of intimacy has remained consistent. Creating Beyoncé World through intimacy now informs her articulation of authenticity.

There has been consistent discourse on the authenticity of rock and the inauthenticity of pop within popular and academic circles since the birth of rock-and-roll. This authentic/inauthentic binary can largely be traced back to Theodor Adorno's (1990) dismissal of popular music and his argument that commodification resulting from commercialisation was in opposition to the essentials of art (Phillips, 1997, p. 144). Simon Frith (1996) is the most vocal in dismissing this authentic/inauthentic binary as redundant, arguing that all genres of music are a performance and can be intended and received as both inauthentic and authentic. David Tetzlaff (1994, p. 111) counters Frith's position by arguing that while a critical stance on the authentic/inauthentic binary is useful, the binary should not be dismissed altogether because of the way it is used by fans. While this chapter follows Frith's assertion that all authenticity is constructed, authenticity still offers a way for fans to evaluate and create meanings around popular music, singing performances and stars, as well as the texts that present them.

Authenticity, and its associated concepts of transparency and intimacy, is also still widely discussed in celebrity studies. Melissa Avdeeff (2016, p. 109), while discussing Beyoncé's Instagram account, argues that 'it is widely accepted that those who engage with celebrities through social media expect a certain degree of authenticity in the form of transparency between the celebrity and their posts'. I would argue this expectation now extends to some degree to music videos, particularly for Beyoncé. Music video audiences automatically search for authenticity or 'truth' in the singer and the image; that is, they search for *Lemonade*'s connection with the 'real' Beyoncé, her life events and her 'real' feelings. This is what Dyer (1986, p. 2) argues cements the whole notion of the star and their appeal: what they 'really are', their inner private self outside their performances. The search for the authentic Beyoncé is futile, but Beyoncé must constantly work to make herself appear authentic in a variety of ways. Jaap Kooijman

(2014, p. 2) argues that the authenticity of African-American female pop stars as saleable commodities is 'doubly questioned, in relation to the predominantly white rock aesthetic as well as music genres such as soul, R&B, and hip-hop that are connoted as "black"'. Beyoncé's strategy for this is the ongoing construction and maintenance of a world that is informed by intimate details of her life and, more so recently, explicitly connected to her gender and racial politics. The more intimate, personal and connected to her real biography, the more authentic the world and, by extension, our view of Beyoncé becomes.

Therefore, elements of Beyoncé's biography lend authenticity to *Lemonade*. Documentary home footage of Beyoncé and Jay-Z's wedding, her pregnancy, her daughter Blue Ivy, her mother's wedding and her interactions with her father when she was a child all infuse *Lemonade* with intimacy and subsequent authenticity. These mirror the images uploaded to her Instagram, Facebook and website, and this level of intimacy is standard practice for social media users. There is a growing area of research into how the presentation of the self on social media has influenced celebrity practice, particularly in reference to Erving Goffman's (1959) book *The Presentation of Self in Everyday Life*. P. David Marshall (2010, p. 44) argues that celebrities use social media to produce the 'public private self', or an intimate yet controlled version of themselves for consumption and apparent social networking. That is, Beyoncé and her team attempt to remain authentic, intimate, personal and offhand, while in fact actively curating and constructing Beyoncé World. It is interesting how much Beyoncé's worlding involves incorporating practices of intimacy common on social media into her professional music videos and visual albums. This blurring between social media and music video reflects the cross-content flows of the contemporary convergent media environment in which boundaries between media forms, aesthetics, genres and technologies are largely breaking down.

A large part of the popular discussion of *Lemonade* focused on the way it addresses ongoing rumours about Jay-Z's infidelity.[13] Whether Jay-Z did or did not cheat on Beyoncé is irrelevant; the way the couple deals with rumours indirectly through their music, rather than any magazine interview or official statement, is testament to their business acumen and their strategies of worlding.[14] Perkins (2005, p. 20) argues that although

---

13   See, for example, Miller (2016), Morris (2016) and Roschke (2016).
14   Jay-Z has now released a response album to *Lemonade*, title *4:44* (2017).

some elements of a film world may mark it as fictional, such as the embodiment of characters by Beyoncé and Jay-Z in *Lemonade*, they 'do not thereby negate its worldhood'. Simon Frith (1996) outlines the different levels of characterisation and narrative in popular song performance:

> There is, first of all, the character presented as the protagonist of the song, its singer and narrator, the implied person controlling the plot, with an attitude and tone of voice; but there may also be a 'quoted' character, the person whom the song is about … On top of this there is the character of the singer as star, what we know about them, or are led to believe about them through their packaging and publicity, and then, further, an understanding of the singer as a person, what we like to imagine they are really like, what is revealed, *in the end*, by their voice. (pp. 198–199, emphasis in original)

Therefore, this layering of characterisation common to pop music performance enhances the worldhood of *Lemonade* and Beyoncé World. *Lemonade* teases the promise of intimacy through its construction of Beyoncé World; it is meant to feel like we are really watching Beyoncé lose her temper at Jay-Z. Because of multiple authorship and address positions in popular song and video, however, *Lemonade* is also a universal statement about all women with cheating husbands, and so the album reveals nothing concrete. The delicate relationship between autobiography and fantasy in *Lemonade*, and Beyoncé's control of this balance to create Beyoncé World, is what makes her star project so interesting in the contemporary moment.

Conclusion

This chapter has argued that Beyoncé's negotiation of stardom is now a strategy of constructing, maintaining and occupying Beyoncé World. Through examining the worlding processes in *Lemonade*, I have outlined the ways in which Beyoncé World is connected to Beyoncé's stardom and articulation of authenticity. Beyoncé World is achieved by both her artistic and professional output and the audience's knowledge of, immersion and participation in her worlding. The audience is aware of the processes of presentation of Beyoncé World, and is actively involved in that world creation through borrowing from the 'real' world. I am in no way suggesting that Beyoncé World is a factual representation of the world or her life. In fact, Beyoncé is well known to have one of the most tightly controlled media strategies in the industry.[15] Instead, this chapter argues that Beyoncé's articulation of authenticity and intimacy, values that have long been critical to celebrity and fame, occurs in a more widespread, encompassing and complex manner than has previously been accounted for. As the lines blur between television, music video, film and music, and if Beyoncé continues to release visual albums, research in pop stardom using theories of film worlds and worlding can only be more productive.

References

Adorno, T. W. 1990. 'On Popular Music', translated by George Simpson. In *On Record: Rock, Pop, and the Written Word*, edited by S. Frith and A. Goodwin, 301–314. London: Routledge.

Avdeeff, M. 2016. 'Beyoncé and Social Media: Authenticity and the Presentation of Self'. In *The Beyoncé Effect: Essays on Sexuality, Race and Feminism*, edited by A. Trier-Bieniek, 109–123. Jefferson: McFarland & Company.

Azzopardi, C. 2014. 'Q&A: Annie Lennox On Her Legacy, Why Beyoncé Is "Feminist Lite"'. *Pride Source*, 25 September. pridesource.com/article.html?article=68228 (accessed 14 July 2017).

Baraka, A. 2016. 'Beyoncé and the Politics of Cultural Dominance'. *Counterpunch*, 11 February. counterpunch.org/2016/02/11/beyonce-and-the-politics-of-cultural-dominance/ (accessed 17 July 2017).

Beebe, R. and J. Middleton (eds). 2007. *Medium Cool: Music Videos from Soundies to Cellphones*. Durham and London: Duke University Press. doi.org/10.1215/9780822390206

Burke, E., B. Knowles-Carter and I. Y. Benatar. 2013. *Beyoncé: Life is but a Dream*. HBO, 16 February. Parkwood Entertainment.

Carter, S. 2017. *4:44*. Roc Nation.

Chatman, D. 2015. 'Pregnancy, Then It's "Back to Business"'. *Feminist Media Studies* 15 (6): 926–941. doi.org/10.1080/14680777.2015.1036901

---

15 In an interview with GQ magazine, Beyoncé revealed she has a personal digital storage archive of her media images, and a visual director who records every moment of her life (see Wallace, 2013).

Clark, N. 2016. 'From Generations of Infidelity and Pain, Beyoncé Makes "Lemonade"'. *The Conversation*, 27 April. theconversation.com/fromgenerations-of-infidelity-and-pain-beyonce-makes-lemonade-58396 (accessed 14 July 2017).

Durham, A. 2012. '"Check on It": Beyoncé, Southern Booty, and Black Femininities in Music Video'. *Feminist Media Studies* 12 (1): 35–49. doi.org/10.1080/14680777.2011.558346

Durham, A., B. C. Cooper and S. M. Morris. 2013. 'The Stage Hip-Hop Feminism Built: A New Directions Essay'. *Signs: Journal of Women in Culture and Society* 38 (3): 721–737. doi.org/10.1086/668843

Dyer, R. 1986. *Heavenly Bodies: Film Stars and Society*. London: Macmillan Education.

———. 1998. *Stars*. New edition with a supplementary chapter and bibliography by Paul McDonald. London: British Film Institute. Original edition, 1979.

Forbes. 2017. 'Beyoncé's net worth: $350 million in 2017'. *Forbes*, 6 June. forbes.com/sites/zackomalleygreenburg/2017/06/06/beyonces-net-worth-350-million-in-2017/#16b3e0786e80 (accessed 17 July 2017).

Frith, S. 1996. *Performing Rites: On the Value of Popular Music*. Cambridge: Harvard University Press.

Frith, S., A. Goodwin and L. Grossberg (eds). 1993. *Sound and Vision: The Music Video Reader*. London; New York: Routledge.

Goffman, E. 1959. *The Presentation of Self in Everyday Life*. New York: Doubleday.

Goodwin, A. 1992. *Dancing in the Distraction Factory: Music Television and Popular Culture*. Minneapolis: University of Minnesota Press.

Griffin, F. J. 2011. 'At Last … ?: Michelle Obama, Beyoncé, Race & History'. *Daedalus* 140 (1): 131–141. doi.org/10.1162/DAED_a_00065

Heinzerling, Z. 2013. *Self-Titled, Part 1*. Columbia Records. youtube.com/watch?v=IcN6Ke2V-rQ (accessed 14 July 2017).

Holmes, S. and S. Redmond. 2006. 'Introduction: Understanding Celebrity Culture'. In *Framing Celebrity: New Directions in Celebrity Culture*, edited by S. Holmes and S. Redmond, 1–16. Oxon; New York: Routledge. doi.org/10.1215/9780822387732-001

James, R. 2008. '"Robo-Diva R&B": Aesthetics, Politics, and Black Female Robots in Contemporary Popular Music'. *Journal of Popular Music Studies* 20 (4): 402–423. doi.org/10.1111/j.1533-1598.2008.00171.x

Jones, L. 2016. 'According to Nielsen SoundScan, A Breakdown of Beyoncé's US & Worldwide Album Sales'. *Huffington Post*, 13 November. huffingtonpost.com/entry/according-to-nielsen-sound scan-a-breakdown-of-beyonces_us_58288b10e4b02b1f5257a471 (accessed 17 July 2017).

Kaplan, E. A. 1987. *Rocking Around the Clock: Music Television, Postmodernism, and Consumer Culture*. New York: Methuen.

Kennedy, G. D. 2011. 'Beyoncé Severs Management Ties with Father'. *Los Angeles Times*, 28 March. latimesblogs.latimes.com/music_blog/2011/03/beyonce-severes-ties-management-ties-with-father.html (accessed 14 July 2017).

Knowles-Carter, B. 2008. *I Am ... Sasha Fierce*. Columbia/Music World.

———. 2013. *Beyoncé*. Columbia/Parkwood Entertainment.

———. 2016a. *Lemonade*. Columbia/Parkwood Entertainment.

———. 2016b. 'Freedom', 7 July. beyonce.com/freedom/ (accessed 17 July 2017).

Kooijman, J. 2014. 'The True Voice of Whitney Houston: Commodification, Authenticity, and African American superstardom'. *Celebrity Studies* 5 (3): 305–320. doi.org/10.1080/19392397.2014.9 11110

Lockett, D., A. Weatherford and L. Peoples. 2016. 'Beyoncé's Lemonade and the Undeniable Power of a Black Woman's Vulnerability'. *Vulture*, 24 April. vulture.com/2016/04/roundtable-beyoncs-lemonade-and-vulnerability.html (accessed 14 July 2017).

London, D. 2016. 'Beyoncé's Capitalism, Masquerading as Radical Change'. *Death and Taxes*, 9 February. web.archive.org/web/20171117011103/https://www.deathandtaxesmag.com/280129/beyonce-capitalism-black-activism/ (accessed 21 July 2017).

Marshall, P. D. 2010. 'The Promotion and Presentation of the Self: Celebrity as Marker of Presentational Media'. *Celebrity Studies* 1 (1): 35–48. doi.org/10.1080/19392390903519057

Miller, J. 2016. 'What Does Jay Z Think of Beyoncé's Lemonade?'. *Vanity Fair*, 27 April. vanityfair.com/hollywood/2016/04/beyonce-lemonade-jay-z (accessed 14 July 2017).

Morris, W. 2016. 'Beyoncé Unearths Pain and Lets It Flow in "Lemonade"'. *The New York Times*, 24 April. nytimes.com/2016/04/25/arts/music/beyonce-unearths-pain-and-lets-it-flow-in-lemonade.html (accessed 14 July 2017).

Oluo, I. 2016. 'Beyoncé's Lemonade is About Much More Than Infidelity and Jay Z'. *The Guardian*, 26 April. theguardian.com/commentisfree/2016/apr/25/beyonce-lemonade-jay-z-infidelity-emotional-project-depths (accessed 14 July 2017).

Perkins, V. F. 2005. 'Where is the World? The Horizon of Events in Movie Fiction'. In *Style and Meaning: Studies in the Detailed Analysis of Film*, edited by J. Gibbs and D. Pye, 16–41. Manchester; New York: Manchester University Press.

Perrott, L., H. Rogers and C. Vernallis. 2016. 'Beyoncé's Lemonade: She Dreams in Both Worlds'. Film International, 2 June. filmint.nu/?p=18413 (accessed 17 July 2017).

Phillips, D. 1997. *Exhibiting Authenticity*. Manchester; New York: Manchester University Press.

Roschke, R. 2016. 'A Step-by-Step Breakdown of the Lemonade Between Beyoncé, Rachel Roy, and Jay Z'. *Pop Sugar*, 26 April. popsugar.com.au/celebrity/Did-Jay-Z-Cheat-Beyonce-Rachel-Roy-41067444#interstitial-0 (accessed 14 July 2017).

Sieczkowski, C. 2014. 'Feminist Activist Says Beyoncé Is Partly "Anti-Feminist" And "Terrorist"'. *Huffington Post*, 10 May huffingtonpost.com.au/entry/beyonce-anti-feminist_n_5295891 (accessed 14 July 2017).

Tetzlaff, D. 1994. 'Music for Meaning: Reading the Discourse of Authenticity in Rock'. *Journal of Communication Inquiry* 18 (1): 95–117. doi.org/10.1177/019685999401800106

Trier-Bieniek, A. (ed.). 2016. *The Beyoncé Effect: Essays on Sexuality, Race and Feminism*. Jefferson, North Carolina: McFarland & Company.

Vernallis, C. 2004. *Experiencing Music Video: Aesthetics and Cultural Context*. New York, Chichester: Columbia University Press.

Wallace, A. 2013. 'Miss Millennium: Beyoncé'. *GQ*, 10 January. gq.com/story/beyonce-cover-story-interview-gq-february-2013 (accessed 14 July 2017).

Weidhase, N. 2015. '"Beyoncé Feminism" and the Contestation of the Black Feminist Body'. *Celebrity Studies* 6 (1): 128–131. doi.org/10.1080/19392397.2015.1005389

Yacavone, D. 2008. 'Towards a Theory of Film Worlds'. *Film-Philosophy* 12 (2): 83–108. doi.org/10.3366/film.2008.0017

———. 2012. 'Spaces, Gaps, and Levels: From the Diegetic to the Aesthetic in Film Theory'. *Music, Sound & the Moving Image* 6 (1): 21–37. doi.org/10.3828/msmi.2012.4

———. 2015. *Film Worlds: A Philosophical Aesthetics of Cinema*. New York: Columbia University Press.

Index

Page numbers in *italic* indicate illustrations. Footnotes are indicated thus: '22n1' (page number, followed by note number).

Abbott, L., 43–4, 49n11, 51
adeptus and its acquisition, 23–4, 29, 30, 32–3
Adler, Moshe, 7
Adorno, T., 118, 145
African-American artists'
    performances in Australia *see* black minstrelsy in Australia
African-American women, 141, 142, 143
Afro-American Minstrel Carnival company *see* Curtis' Afro-American Minstrel Carnival company
'Alexander's Ragtime Band' (Hugo company performance), 49–50
Allen, Richard 'Pistol', 99
Amphlett, Chrissy, 15–16, 74, 82
Arena, Tina, 82
Art Worlds (Becker), 22
Ashford, Jack, 103
Astor Records, 61
asynchrony, fruitful, 28, 29, 32
Australian circus bands, 45, 47
Australian Gay Rights movement, 84
Australian jazz, 15, 40–1, 58
    contribution of African-American musicians, 15, 39, 49–51
    Jacques and, 15, 56–8, 64
    see also black minstrelsy in Australia; jazz music

Australian Jazz Bell Awards, 64
Australian popular music, 15–16, 57–8, 76–8
    Jacques and *see* Jacques, Judy
    Saddington and *see* Saddington, Wendy
'Australia's First Jazz Band', 40, 41, 49
auteurs/auteurship, 8, 9, 10, 12–13
authentic music, 130, 145
authenticity, notions of, 8, 9, 130–2, 138, 145–6, 147, 148
Avdeeff, Melissa, 145
Axiom (band), 77
Aztecs, The (band), 77, 81–2

Bacharach, Burt, 60, 62
backing bands, 16, 82, 100–3, 111
    Funk Brothers, 96–100, 111
    Wrecking Crew, 101
    see also Soul Sundays (recording project)
Barcelona (album), 16–17, 115–16, 120–32
    influences, 128
    reception of, 115, 116, 122, 131–2
    single releases, 129
    vocal, instrumental and production devices, 123–30
'Barcelona' (song), 16, 121, 124–7, 129

Bayly, Mark, 86
Beach Boys, The, 101
Becker, H. *see Art Worlds* (Becker)
Beghetto, R. A., 21
Benjamin, Rick, 45
Benjamin, William 'Benny', 99–100
Berlin, Irving, 50
Berresford, M., 39, 40, 47
Berry, Chuck, 6, 96
Beyoncé
    artistic and commercial achievements, 138
    and contemporary media environment, 140–1
    cultural and racial heritage, 143
    negotiation of race, sexuality and gender, 141, 142, 143
    public private self, 144–6
    worlding (Beyoncé World), 11, 17, 137–48
Beyoncé (album), 137, 145
Black Lives Matter movement, 141, 142
black minstrelsy in Australia, 15, 39, 41–51
    bands and orchestras, 43, 44–9
    comedic appeal, 41, 42, 43–4, 47, 48
    contribution to Australian jazz, 15, 39, 44, 49–51
    'Georgia' companies, *37*, 42–8
    racist attitudes to, 49, 50
    ragging and ragtime, 41, 42, 43, 44–5, 47–50
black music, 38–41, 58, 59–60, 146
Black Nativity (*Go Tell it on the Mountain*) cast, 59–60
black women, 141, 142, 143
blackface (white) minstrelsy, 38, 41–2, 45
Boden, M., 22n1, 31, 32
'Bohemian Rhapsody' (song), 16, 119–20, 128, 131
    vocal, instrumental and production devices, 123–7

Bolden, Buddy, 45
Bonner, Frances, 4
Bourdieu, P., 22, 22n1, 23
Bradford, Alex, 59–60
Braithwaite, Daryl, 82
brass bands, 43, 44–9
Brian Brown Ensemble, 64
Brisbane Jam Fam, 97, 105
Brown, Billy, 44
Brown, Brian, 64
Brown, Eric, 57
Brown, J. J., 83
'bubblegum' musicians, 77
Burns, Ronnie, 61

Caballé, Montserrat, 120–1
    collaboration with Mercury, 16, 116, 120–32
    vocal devices in repertory opera and *Barcelona*, 116, 123–30, 131
cakewalk-style minstrelsy and music, 43, 44, 45, 47, 48 *see also* black minstrelsy in Australia
Campelo, I., 102
canon formation, 9–10
canonisation of music artists, 10–12
Carmen, Loene, 73, 74, 87
Carter, Shawn (Jay-Z) *see* Jay-Z (Shawn Carter)
Caruso, Enrico, 117, 118
celebrity, 2–6
    authenticity and, 145–6
    branding, 60
    diversity of types, 11
    renown and, 2, 5
    social media and celebrity practice, 146
    see also stardom
Celebrity and Power: Fame in Contemporary Culture (Marshall), 9
Celebrity Studies (journal), 5
Chain (band), 77, 81–2, 84 *see also* Saddington, Wendy

Chlopicki, I. T., 83–4
circus sideshow bands, 39–40, 45, 47
Clarke, Leah, 49, 50
classical music, 117–19, 128
Clay, Sonny, 40
Clifton Hill Community Music Centre, 63
Colored Idea Company, 40, 49, 50
consumer identification with stars, 7–9
'coon-song', 43, 45, 48
Copperwine (band), 77, 78, 82
Corby, Sheraden, 15, 43, 44
Countdown (television program), 82
creativity
    capacity to be creative, 30
    creative propulsion, 28–9, 31–2
    cross-disciplinary skills (field switching), 29–30, 32
    definitions and terminologies, 22n1
    model of creative magnitude, 21, 23
    qualities of the creative personality, 31–2
    systems model of creativity, 14, 22, 28, 31
    'triangle of creativity', 28
creativity in songwriting
    characteristics of the very best songwriters, 24–5, 33
    factors influencing, 14, 23–33
    lessons for songwriters, 22
    models of creativity, 21–3, 28, 31
    paradigm-shifting creativity, 14, 30–3
    significant works, 27, 30–1
Crest record label, 58, 59
crime conviction impact on cultural status of stars, 11
crossover music
    opera–popular music, 116, 117–19, 132
Crozier, Jeff, 80

Crusoe, Billy, 44
Csikszentmihalyi, Mihaly, 14, 22, 28
Curtis' Afro-American Minstrel Carnival company, 43, 47–9

Daddy Cool (band), 77
Day, T., 117–18
Death and the Rock Star (Strong and Lebrun), 10–11
death of artist, impact on star status, 10–11
Detroit recording industry *see* Motown
Dilverd, Thomas (Japanese Tommy), 44
discriminant pattern recognition, 24–5, 30
Divinyls (band) *see* Amphlett, Chrissy
Dolenz, Mickey, 101
Donati, Sandro, 65
Drysdale, Denise, 77
Duffett, Mark, 13
Durbin, Alison, 77
Dyer, Richard, 2–3, 4, 137, 145
Dylan, Bob, 59

Easton, Hosea, 44
Eden, Karise, 74
Edinburgh Festival Fringe 1997, 64
Emerson, K., 96
Engleheart, Murray, 81
expert variation and selective retention in creativity, 30
expertise *see* adeptus and its acquisition

'fallen' star metaphors, 11
Fame Games (Turner, Bonner and Marshall), 4
Farnham, Johnny, 77, 81
female musicians *see* women musicians
feminism
    Beyoncé and, 141, 142
    Saddington and, 84

field switching and creativity, 29–30, 32
film industry, stardom in, 2–3, 5, 6
film theory, 139
'film world' concept, 139, 141 *see also* worlding and worldhood
Flinders Island, 65
folk music, 58, 59
Foo Fighters (band), 12
'Formation' (song), 142, 143
Forster, Robert, 74
Franklin, Aretha, 60, 77, 78, 79
Frith, S., 60, 63, 145, 147
Funk Brothers, 16, 96–100, 111
    research project related to, 16, 97–8, 102–12

Garbutt, Maurice, 58
Gardner, Howard, 22n1, 25, 26, 28
Gebert, Bobby, 82
gender inequality
    within cultural industries, 11
    in music industry, 57–8, 74, 77, 81, 82, 88
    see also male musicians; women musicians
George, Linda, 77
George, N., 97, 99
'Georgia' companies, *37*, 42–8 *see also* black minstrelsy in Australia
Geraghty, Christine, 4–5
Geyer, Renée, 74, 77
Gillespie, Dizzy, 64
Gledhill, Christine, 3
Glitter, Gary, 11
Go Tell it on the Mountain (*Black Nativity*) cast, 59–60
Go-Betweens (band), 74
Gordy, Berry, 16, 95–6, 98
Go-Set (magazine), 77, 80–1, 82, 83, 84, 87
Gospel Four, The (band), 59, 66
gospel singing, 59–60, 66–7
Grohl, Dave, 12
Guilliatt, Richard, 81

habitus *see* adeptus and its acquisition
Handy, W. C., 40
Hare Krishna Band, 78, 82
Hare Krishna movement, 85, 87
Harrison, C. M., 24, 25, 29–30, 32
Head, Peter, 82, 85, 87
Heavenly Bodies: Film Stars and Society (Dyer), 3
Herman, Marcus, 58
Hicks, Charles B., 37, 43, 44
Hicks-Sawyer Minstrels, 15, 43, 44, 45, 46, 47
hidden musicians, 11, 16, 74, 102, 111–12 *see also* backing bands; session musicians; women musicians
historiography, 11, 39–40, 74–6
Hitsville USA, 16, 96, 98–9
Hogan, Ernest, 44, 48
Holmes, Su, 2, 9, 138
house bands *see* backing bands
Hugo's Colored Minstrels, 15, 43, 49, 50

'identity politics' of stardom, 4, 5
Idlers Five, The (band), 61
Impiombato, Nathan, 61n6, 66
Indecent Exposures. Twenty Years of Australian Feminist Photography (Moore), 84
Inglis, Fred, 2, 5
intelligence
    multiple intelligence theory, 25, 31
    naturalistic, 25–6
International Association for the Study of Popular Music (IASPM), Australia and New Zealand branch conference 2015, 13–14

Jackson, Mahalia, 79
Jackson, Michael, 7
Jacques, Judy, 11, 15, 55–68, *57*, *61*, *67*

INDEX

experimental music, 56, 63–4, 68
gospel pioneering, 59–60
jazz music, 56–8, 64
and local community, 57, 65
pop commodity, 60–3
popular music industry, independence from, 11, 15, 55–6, 63, 68
recordings, 58, 59, 61, 66–7
soul music, 62, 66
Jamerson, James, 99, 100
James, Harvey, 82
James Taylor Move (band), 77, 82
Japanese Tommy (Thomas Dilverd), 44
Jay-Z (Shawn Carter), 144, 146–7
Jazz (documentary), 38
jazz music
historiography, 39–40, 45
terminology, 39, 40–1
jazz music, Australian, 15, 40–1, 58
contribution of African-American musicians, 15, 39, 49–51
Jacques and, 15, 56–8, 64
in Melbourne, 58
see also black minstrelsy in Australia
jazzing, 40, 41, 44–5, 49
Jerrems, Carol, 84
Jones, Uriel, 99–100
Joplin, Janis, 78
Jorgenson, Sigmund, 64
'jubilee' companies *see* black minstrelsy in Australia
Judy Jacques Ensemble, 64
Judy Jacques' Lighthouse, 64 *see also* Jacques, Judy
Justman, P., 103

Kansas City Pickaninny Band, 47–9
Kaufman, J. C., 21, 22n1, 26, 27
Keenan, Sam, 44
Kersands, Billy, 44, 49
Kevin Borich Express, 78, 82

Kilby, Jordie and David, 59
Knowles-Carter, Beyoncé *see* Beyoncé
Kooijman, Jaap, 145–6

Lacan, Jacques, 38, 39, 50
Lah De Dahs (band), 77
Langdon, David, 62
Lanza, Mario, 117, 118, 119
Lebrun, Barbara, 10–11
Lemonade (visual album), 17, 138–47
Lena, J. C., 26
Lennon, John, 27
Lewis, Steven, 40
Liber, Mick, 82
Little, Jeannie, 77
live performance, aura elicited by musicians in, 13
Lloyd, Lobby, 82
Long Way to the Top (television series), 79
Los Angeles recording industry, 101
Loudin's Fisk Jubilee Singers, 43
Lozito, C., 96–7, 100
Lying Up a Nation: Race and Black Music (Radano), 38–9

McAdoo minstrel companies, 43, 46, 47
McAdoo, Orpheus, 43
McAskill, Barry, 82
McClain, Billy, 44
McIntyre, Iain, 78, 83
McIntyre, P., 22, 22n1
McKenna, Des, 82
MacLean, Stephen, 79, 87
McLeod, K., 119–20, 131
male musicians
privileging of, 77, 81, 88
Saddington collaboration with, 82, 84, 85
see also gender inequality
Maloney, Peter, 86
Manchester, UK, 62
Manning, Phil, 85

157

Marshall, P. David, 4, 9, 146
Martha and the Vandellas (band), 96, 99
Martin, Max, 27
'master signifier' words, 38
Mastodon Colored Minstrels, 43, 44
Max Merritt and the Meteors (band), 77
May, Brian, 119
May, Ida, 44
'media texts' and construction of star image, 3, 4–5, 137, 144
Melbourne, 58, 59
Meldrum, Ian 'Molly', 82
Mercury, Freddie, 119
   collaboration with Caballé, 16, 116, 120–32
   musical and vocal devices in *Barcelona* and 'Bohemian Rhapsody', 116, 123–30, 131
   vocal characteristics, 121, 129–30
Merritt, Max, 77, 82
Minogue, Kylie, 82, 86
minstrel shows, 39–40, 42
   in Australia *see* black minstrelsy in Australia
   blackface, 38, 41–2, 45
   comedic appeal, 41, 42, 43–4, 47, 48
   jazz-antecedent practices, 42
   ragging and ragtime, 41, 42, 43, 44–5, 47–50
models of creativity
   applied, 23–33
   model of creative magnitude, 21, 23
   systems model of creativity, 14, 22, 28, 31
Monkees, The, 101
Moon, Keith, 82
Moore, A., 130–2
Moore, Catriona, 84
Moran, Mike, 121, 122, 128, 129n8, 132

Morgan, Warren, 80n6, 82
Morton, D., 116n1
Motown, 95–7
   drum beat, 99
   Hitsville USA, 16, 96, 98–9
   key instrumentalists, 98–100
   recording processes, 103
   rhythm section beds, 96, 111
   see also Funk Brothers; *Soul Sundays* (recording project)
multiple intelligence theory, 25, 31
music festivals, 79, 81, 87
music magazines, 87
   Go-Set, 77, 80–1, 82, 83, 84
music technology stars, 12 *see also* recording technologies
music video scholarship, 139
music videos, 138, 139–40, 145, 146
   see also visual albums
musical legacies of women musicians, 15–16, 73–4, 86, 87

naturalistic intelligence, 25–6
'Negro spiritual' companies *see* black minstrelsy in Australia
Neve, Rupert, 12
New Orleans and the origins of jazz, 39–40, 45
Newton-John, Olivia, 77
Northern Soul music, 15, 62, 66

O'Keefe, Johnny, 60–1
opera
   authenticity, 130–2
   Barcelona collaboration between Mercury and Caballé, 16–17, 120–32
   Tommy (rock opera), 82
   within popular culture, 16–17, 116–20
Orgeron, Marsha, 2, 4, 5
Original Georgia Minstrels (touring company), 15, *37*, 43

parade bands, 44–9
pattern recognition, discriminant, 24–5, 30
Perkins, V. F., 139, 144, 146–7
'personality' (term), 2
Peter, Paul and Mary (band), 59
Peterson, R. A., 26
Pickaninny Band, 47–9
Plantation Orchestra, 40, 50
Playback Records, 66–7
Playing Ad Lib, Improvisatory Music in Australia: 1836–1970 (Whiteoak), 40
Poetics of Rock: Cutting Tracks, Making Records, The (Zak III), 102
pop music (genre)
    authenticity/inauthenticity, 145–6
    'bubblegum' musicians, 77
    historiography, 11
    Jacques and, 60–2
    Max Martin contribution, 27
    'queens of pop', 77
    rejection/dismissal of (1970s), 76, 77
Pope, Charlie, 44
popular music
    characterisation and narrative in popular song performance, 147
    opera within popular recording cultures, 16–17, 116–20
    reality television shows, 12–13
    role of backing bands, 16, 96–103, 111
    stardom in, 6–17, 60–1, 77
    see also stardom
    vocal style and production, 118–19
popular music, Australian 1970s, 76–8
    Jacques and, 60–2
    Saddington and, 76, 77, 78–9, 82–3
posthumous canonisation of music artists, 10–11

Presley, Elvis, 6, 56, 101
Pretz, J. E., 26, 27
productivity (creators), 26–7
'progressive rock' musicians, 77
propulsion, creative, 28–9, 31–2

Queen (band), 115, 119–20, 121
    see also Mercury, Freddie

Radano, Ronald, 15, 38–9
radio shows, 61, 66
Ragged but Right (Abbott and Seroff), 44
ragging and ragtime, 41, 42, 43, 44–5, 47–50
RareCollections (radio show), 59, 66
'the real', Lacan's theory of, 38, 39, 50
recording aesthetics, 119
recording cultures, defined, 116n1
recording spaces/studios, 97, 103–4, 107, 110–11
recording technologies, 12, 97
    and audience engagement with classical music, 117–18, 119
    used in *Soul Sunday* project, 104, 108
Redmond, Sean, 2, 138
renown and celebrity, 2, 5 *see also* stardom
Revolution, The (band), 77, 82
rhythm-and-blues music, 62, 95, 96
    see also Motown; Saddington, Wendy
risk-taking in songwriting, 29, 32
RoadKnight, Margret, 59, 60, 77
Rock & Roll Hall of Fame and Museum, Cleveland, 10
'Rock Chicks' (Icon exhibition, 2010), 86
rock music, 10–11, 76–8
    authenticity, 130–2, 145–6
    Barcelona collaboration between Mercury and Caballé, 16–17, 120–32

gender inequality in, 74, 77, 81, 82, 88
historiography, 11
'progressive rock' musicians, 77
rock values, 10
'rockers' versus 'jazzers', 58n3
sub-genres, 76
Tommy (rock opera), 82
women musicians, 74–6, 77
see also Saddington, Wendy
Rylands, Billy, 82

Saddington, Wendy, *76*
  Australian popular music and, 76, 77, 78–9, 82–3
  career, 11, 15–16, 78–81, 86
  collaboration with other musicians, 77–8, 82, 84, 85
  death, 73, 87
  influence on others, 74, 84, 85
  influences on, 15, 78, 79, 80
  journalism, 80–1, 84, 87
  legacy, 15–16, 74, 77, 86, 87
  live performances, 79, 82, 85, 87
  looks, style and personality, 16, 83–5, 87–8
  recordings, 78, 79, 82
  songwriting, 79–80
  television shows and film, 78–9
  tributes to, 73, 77–8, 82–3, 87
  'Underground Icon' exhibition, 16, 85–6
  see also Chain (band)
Sales, Irving, 44, 47
'Sasha Fierce' persona, 144–5 *see also* Beyoncé
Sawyer, R. K., 22n1, 26, 27, 29, 30–1
Scott, D., 130
Seekers, The , 58
Seroff, D., 43–4, 49n11, 51
session musicians, 96–103, 111 *see also* backing bands
A Short History of Celebrity (Inglis), 2, 5

Shuker, Roy, 8–9
Shumway, David R., 6
significant works, 27, 30–1
Simone, Nina, 78, 79
Simonton, Dean Keith, 22n1
Sinatra, Frank, 6, 101
Sinatra, Nancy, 101
Skyhooks (band), 77
Slutsky, A., 99
Smith, Broderick, 82
Smith, Henderson, 47, 48
Smith, Nathaniel Clark, 47, 48
social media, 5, 11, 141
  Beyoncé and, 138, 144, 145, 146
  celebrity practice and, 146
song lineage and antecedents, 26
songwriting and songwriters
  characteristics of the very best songwriters, 24–5, 31–3
  factors influencing creativity, 14, 23–33
  lessons for songwriters, 22
  methodology, 31–3
  models of creativity, 21–3
  paradigm-shifting creativity, 14, 30–3
  significant works, 27, 30–1
Sonny and Cher, 101
soul music, 60, 62, 76–8, 79, 95
  Motown success, 95–7, 99 *see also* Funk Brothers
  Northern Soul, 15, 62, 66
  see also gospel singing
Soul Sundays (recording project), 16, 97–8, 102–12
  collaborators, 105–6, *107*
  instruments and equipment, 104, 105, 106, 107–8
  method, 105–8
  results and reflections, 108–10
Sound City (Grohl, Rota and Ramsay), 12
Sousa band, 45
Spector, Phil, 101

Speed, Billy, 44
St John, Jeff, 77, 78, 83, 84, 85
stardom, 1–14
    authenticity and, 8, 9, 130, 145–6, 147, 148
    Beyoncé and, 137–48
    celebrity and, 2–6
    in flux, 15, 55–6, 64
    Jacques and, 11, 15, 55–68
    manufactured, 12–13
    measurement of, 7
    monetary success and, 7
    within popular music industry, 6–17, 60–1, 77
    Saddington and, 11, 15–16, 73–88
    scholarship, 2–14
    star image, 3, 4–5, 6, 137, 138
    technological, 12
    terminology, 1–2, 3, 137
    'work of stardom', 4
    worlding *see* worlding and worldhood
Stardom: Industry of Desire (Gledhill), 3
stars
    auteurship, 8, 9, 10, 12–13
    consumer identification with, 7–9
    death of, 10–11
    'fallen' star metaphors, 11
    'star' definition, 1
    'superstars', 2, 7
Stars (Dyer), 2–3
Sternberg, R. J., 22n1, 26, 27
Stewart, Kathleen, 73
Stomp and Swerve: American Music Gets Hot (Wondrich), 45
Strong, Catherine, 10–11, 74, 77n2, 81, 82
Sunbury (music festival), 81
'superstar' (term), 2, 7
Supremes, The (group), 96, 106
Sweatman, Wilbur C., 47, 48
Sweeney, Chris, 82

Sylvia and the Synthetics, 84
systems model of creativity, 14, 22, 25n2, 28, 31

talent, defined, 55
Tamla Motown *see* Motown
Taylor, Eva, 44
technological stardom, 12 *see also* recording technologies
television shows
    Jacques appearances, 59, 60–1, 66
    reality shows, 12–13
    Saddington appearances, 78–9
Tetzlaff, David, 145
Thistlethwayte, R., 26
Thorpe, Billy, 77, 80, 81, 82
Tommy (rock opera), 82
Toynbee, J., 8
Travers, Mary, 57, 59
Trevi, Gloria, 11
trombone music, 45, 47, 48
True, Everett, 73, 84
Tudor, Ron, 61, 62
Turner, Graeme, 2, 4
Twisted Wheel nightclub, Manchester, 62
Two Jays, The, 56

'Uncle Tom's Cabin' (melodrama), 43
'Underground Icon' exhibition, 2015–16, 16, 85–6
'underground' music, 76, 77
Understanding Celebrity (Turner), 4
Understanding Popular Music Culture (Shuker), 9

Van Dyke, Earl, 99
vaudeville acts, 15, 40, 47, 51
Veith, Barry, 63
Vincent Perry's Motown Revue musicians, 105
visual albums, 140, 146
    Beyoncé, 137, 145
    Lemonade, 17, 138–47
Voice, The, competition, 12, 74

Walker, Charles W., 44
Warwick, Dionne, 60
Warwick, Jacqueline, 7
Was, Don, 100
Watkins, Ian, 11
Weight, Greg, 84
Weisberg, R. W., 22n1, 30
Wendy Saddington Band, 82 *see also* Saddington, Wendy
White Australia policy, 50
Whiteoak, J., 40, 41
Williams, A., 100–1
Wilson, Billy, 44
Wilson, Brian, 101
Wilson, Ross, 82
Winged Messenger (record and jazz/modal opera), 64
Wirth's Circus band, 45
women musicians
    commodification of, 15, 56, 60, 61, 68
    as decoration, 57–8
    exhibitions featuring, 85–6, 87
    legacies, 15–16, 73–4, 86, 87
    mainstream expectations of, 60, 61, 82
    'pioneering role' statements, 73–4
    poorly acknowledged/documented, 11, 74–6
    ragtime music, 49
    rock music, 74, 77
    see also gender inequality; Beyoncé; Jacques, Judy; Saddington, Wendy
Wonder, Stevie, 98, 99, 106
Wondrich, David, 45
words
    Lacan's theory of categories of meaning, 38
'work of stardom', 4
works, significant, 27, 30–1

worlding and worldhood, 138, 139, 144
    Beyoncé's star project, 17, 137, 139–40, 144–8
    Lemonade as case study, 17, 140–4
Wrecking Crew (band), 101
Wyn Jones, Caris, 10

Yacavone, Daniel, 139, 140, 141, 144
Yarra Reunion Band, 64
Yarras, The (Yarra Yarra New Orleans Jazz Band), 56–7, 58, 59, 66
'You're Messin' Up My Mind' (song), 15, 56, 61, 62, 66

Zak III, A. J., 102
Zoot (band), 77

www.ingramcontent.com/pod-product-compliance
Lightning Source LLC
Chambersburg PA
CBHW061247230426
43662CB00021B/2453